What they're saying:

"Here at last, despairing parents, is **help**.
If changing the locks and long vacations didn't work,
this book probably **will**. Her bias falls on the side
of open hearts, open arms, open house."
MINNEAPOLIS STAR TRIBUNE

"A **truly helpful book** to put today's
family problems in perspective."
LOS ANGELES TIMES

"...**recycling nesters** takes lots of work...
and **guidelines** for re-entry into the home need
to be drawn before the grown child arrives
at the door, car filled with dirty laundry."
ST. PETERSBURG TIMES

"...laces **humor with hard facts,**
presents a good case
for young adults living at home
and gives a **bill of rights**
for parents and nesters."
FORT MEYERS NEWS PRESS

"...a very **readable, practical, informative** book
on a growing issue."
BOULDER SUNDAY CAMERA MAGAZINE

"Adult children by the thousands are moving
back home again. Is the rebellion over?
PARADE MAGAZINE

"There are **many reasons** for this surge in the
'nesting in' of grown offspring
and author O'Kane discusses these reasons, along with their
positive and negative results.
She discovered **practical, wise answers.**"
VIRTUE MAGAZINE

"...there is a **potential for problems**
when young adults move back home.
But, the situation may offer mutual companionship
while giving the child a chance to save money."
HARTFORD COURANT

"This book is much needed for parents who have grown
children who still live at home. She adds
spice and humor to many real-life situations
and sees the **positive** in what others may feel
very negative about in their attitudes.
This **inspiring book**
holds your interest."
AUGSBURG NEWSLETTER

"Warm, friendly people with a
common sense attitude
mixed with humor."
HOLLYWOOD (FLORIDA) SUN-TATTLER

"The results of her work shed light on the phenomenon
which is today becoming quite ordinary.
The many suggestions and anecdotes
in Monica O'Kane's book **will be helpful**
to households with adult children.
Living With Adult Children is a welcome addition
to the literature on family life"
LE LECHE LEAGUE INTERNATIONAL'S LEAVEN

"O'Kane suggests basic guidelines for parents concerned
about the long-term effects of their
adult child's living at home."
OUR SUNDAY VISITOR

"What should be the **ground rules** if young adults are
allowed to live at home? This author attempts
a **balanced approach** to these problems
and offers her own and others' experiences
in dealing with this situation."
LIGUORIAN

"O'Kane filled her book with **practical examples**
and solutions for household problems
wrought by 'nesting' children."
MIAMI VOICE

"The book tells of pleasures, problems with nesters.
This is one mother's declaration to her dependents.
FORT WORTH STAR TELEGRAM

"O'Kane points out the positive benefit of 'familyness.' She
reminds the reader that family life
is an accepting relationship,
not a rejecting one."
FLORIDA BAPTIST WITNESS

"...a **most valuable** book. There is nothing like it on the
market. Apple Tree Family Ministries
highly recommends her book to anyone
who has, or contemplates having, adult children
living at home."
APPLE TREE FAMILY MINISTRIES

"...**advice** and **anecdotes** for young adults
and their parents on money, communication,
household chores,
church attendance, and fostering independence."
NATIONAL CATHOLIC NEWS SERVICE

"According to Monica O'Kane, money can be a
major problem encountered by these extended families.
Authority is another powder keg for trouble.
It's a two-way street."
MICHIGAN CATHOLIC

"This author has **spelled out the rules**
and provided **standards and guidance**
for other parents faced with similar situations. "
CATHOLIC BULLETIN,
Minneapolis / St. Paul Archdiocese

"**Compromise** is important. The main problem
is recognizing that kids can be on their own.
They can be talked to
without being given advice.
Call for change
when children 'return to nest.'"
NEWSDAY

"In a **lucid way,** laced with **humor,** the author
approaches this problem area of family life.
This exceptionally **well-written** guide
is **invaluable**
and will benefit all readers."
ARTHUR MANDELBAUM, MSW,
SR. CONSULTANT,
MENNINGER FOUNDATION

"...a how-to-book that freely points out
the **pitfalls** and **opportunities** facing a family
with adult live-in offspring:
it neither sentimentalizes
nor deplores."
ELISE BOULDING, PHD,
CHAIRMAN, SOCIOLOGY DEPARTMENT,
DARTMOUTH COLLEGE

"I would **highly recommend** this book
to parents, adult children, therapists and
educators working with
adult children and their parents."
PATRICIA BECKLER, MSW,
ASSISTANT PROFESSOR,
COLLEGE OF ST. BENEDICT

Hey, Mom, I'm Home Again!

Strategies for parents and grown children who live together

By Monica Lauen O'Kane

Published by

MARLOR PRESS, INC.

HEY, MOM,
I'M HOME
AGAIN

Published by Marlor Press, Inc.

Cover design by Georgene Sainati
Inside illustrations by Marlin Bree

ISBN 0-943400-68-6

Distributed to the book trade by Contemporary Books, Chicago

Printed in the United States of America

Now revised, updated and expanded, this book
was originally published by Diction Books under the title,
Living With Adult Children.

Disclaimer: This book is intended as a general guide
to practical matters pertaining to family relationships.
Readers should use their own judgement and discretion on individual
applications and seek out medical or other help when appropriate to meet
their own specific needs. This book is not a substitute for professional counseling or medical or other scientific service. In any event, the author and
Marlor Press are not responsible for damages, agreements, facilities,
loss or injury, of any kind.

Marlor Press, Inc.
4304 Brigadoon Drive / Saint Paul, MN 55126

Contents

6/ Communications:
so let's talk about it, 105

Pressure? Tension? Open communications can salvage difficult situations. Here are tips on reading body language, learning to listen, negotiating and, especially, catching on to compromise. Why establishing *house rules* is an advantage—and some examples for you to use.

7/ Money matters—it really does, 129

Should nesters pay room and board? How much? Why and how to talk about practical money problems that bug many nesters, including living within one's means.

8/ Negative attitudes, 159

Here are some strategies to turn negative viewpoints into positive ones. Survival outlooks and attitudes. How to use a target departure date as a technique to help endure an awkward nesting situation.

9/ When nesters choose
different lifestyles, 171

Not every child turns out the way parents expect. In sticky situations, here are ways to share love and respect even though nesters may be going against the family's grain. Includes how to uphold home standards and tips to handle embarrassing problems.

10/ Reroosting: dealing with
returning nesters, 187

Grown children can be independent—and this can cause problems when they return home. Here are strategies and examples to smooth re-entry and give nesters a new sense of appreciation of home life.

Bibliography, 203

Problems

and

solutions

My adult daughter, suitcases in both hands,
just showed up at the front doorstep,
demanding to stay at home again.
What do we do next? *See chapter 6.*

My son has a full-time job and makes an adequate
income. How can I get him to pay his share
of room and board? *See chapter 7.*

My adult daughter is bringing male friends
home to stay overnight.
How can we get our home back
to our family standards? *See chapter 9.*

We argue a lot, and that's very upsetting.
How can we really communicate
with our nesters—and achieve more harmony?
See chapter 6.

Our friends think our son is a bum
for still living at home. What's the answer for us—
how can I respond? *See chapter 8.*

What can we do now that we know
our 26-year-old daughter
is a lesbian? *See chapter 9.*

Dedication

THIS BOOK is dedicated to my family,
who have brought me the widest array of emotions—
peaks, as well as valley days.

They have enabled me to live life to the fullest.
From the time I was five years old, I yearned for the day when
I would marry and have children. I wanted a full life and
didn't ever want to be bored:

to Hugh, my husband,
my friend, my supporter;

to my children: Maureen, Kevin, Tracy, Pat,
Katie, Joe, Tom and Meg;

to my daughters-and sons-in law: Dave,
Terry, Karen, Scott, and Laurie;

to my grandchildren: Mo and Matt, Claire
and Bridget, Kelsey, Rachel and Ryan;

and to those in-laws yet to join the family
and grandchildren yet to be born.

Thank you for saving me
from a life of boredom!

Additionally, I'd also like to dedicate this work
to families everywhere, wishing them happiness
and fulfillment in family relationships.

—*Monica Lauen O'Kane*

Foreword

TEN YEARS AGO, Monica Lauen O'Kane asked me to write a
foreword to her book, *Living With Adult Children*.
It is important to note that Monica was either the first person,
or one of the first people, in the country
to bring our attention to a social phenomenon
that we now recognize is quite common:
children who either don't leave home after high school or
adult children who come back to live in their parents' home.

The American family is in the process of rapid change.
Monica's topic on living with adult children is but one of
these important changes. Other changes are the impact of
mothers working outside the home, the increased role of
fathers in child care, the impact of the worsening economy on
the time available for parenting, and so on.

As the general economy deteriorates in the 1990s,
the number of adult children living in their parents' home will
increase. Hence, the importance of Monica's book will gain
strength in the immediate future.

This book is very readable and is written to every
person. The language used is direct, clear and important.
I predict that the people who do read this book will use it like
the local phone book: it will be used frequently, perhaps
daily, notes will be written on the cover, and in the margins.

Roger Lauen, Ph.D.
Sociologist and Criminologist

Preface

My husband and I have eight children, all now adults. For many years we've had anywhere from one to four of our adult children living at home. The number is constantly fluctuating, but one thing is for sure—there always seems to be one at home, one leaving, or one planning on a return stay. Our eldest, Maureen, has moved in and out so often that she calls herself, "The Yoyo." No wonder some people term this "the swinging door syndrome."

Because of our family situation, I wanted to read something informative about grown children who live at home. But I couldn't find any book written on the subject. I finally concluded that, to read the book, I'd first have to write it.

And why not?

To begin with, our family had plenty of first-hand experience so I knew the questions I wanted answers for. Besides, I love to research topics. So I gathered all the available information the local libraries had to offer—but, unfortunately, it really wasn't what I was looking for.

Most of the published data had been written by professionals, who generally were working with troubled families who had come to them for counsel. But, I wanted information about "normal" families. So I had to set out to find it myself.

A survey seemed the best way to get the data I needed. I sent a carefully worded, seven-page questionnaire to families in many geographical areas, with varying income levels, ethnic backgrounds, and family size. The only prerequisite for participation in the study was that the family include an adult child or children—age 18 or a high school graduate, whichever came later—living in the parental home.

Survey respondents were from a wide range of families as follows:

- Financial status: A combined parental income from $14,00 to $100,000 annually.
- Ethnic groups: Caucasian, Lebanese, Hawaiian, Black, Canadian, Mexican.
- Family size: From one to 11 children per family.
- Geographical area: Colorado, Florida, Hawaii, Illinois, Indiana, Iowa, Minnesota, New Jersey, New York, Ohio, and South Dakota.

I received more than 125 completed surveys. Sixty-nine had been filled in by one of the parents—most often by the mother, with one step-mother, and some fathers responding. Fifty-four were completed by adult offspring, with five surveys being jointly filled in by both a parent and their offspring, and four completed by both parents together. In 11 instances, both a parent and an adult offspring in the same family responded on separate questionnaires. Additionally, eight individuals granted me face-to-face interviews.

All questionnaire respondents have been given fictitious names, as have the people in the human interest stories used liberally throughout the book. But they are real and alive people—as real as your own family. The only true names used are public figures, such as television personality and talk show host, Phil Donahue, and families and persons who have been featured in newspaper or magazine articles.

It was a delight to read the completed surveys. They came from average, ordinary families trying to work out their situation of having a Full Nest. Reading the completed surveys, therefore, also gave me new encouragement. One mother even replied, "Your survey was interesting, and in answering it, Nellie (her daughter) and I became closer and more open with each other."

Quotations from the surveys are sprinkled throughout the book in hopes of giving you, the reader, a glimpse of what I saw while reading them. Included in this book are examples of various situations from these families and their reactions.

It is my belief that, with the examples of others who have made it work, this book will give encouragement and understanding to those families who have their adult children living at home.

It must be added that my husband and I grew up in homes where God played a daily part, and we are deeply committed to a religious philosophy. We feel that it is only with the daily help of the Lord that we can fulfill our duties as parents. But, being spiritual doesn't mean there won't be problems. It does mean, however, that God will help us with them. We trust, rely on, and acknowledge our need for His help. On countless occasions, He has been our source of strength. Many times a day, an arrow prayer to heaven brings a quick response.

This book was originally published in 1981. Following publication, I was most gratified by the many letters and phone calls from people who said they appreciated the book and were helped by it. Two of the most effective interviews, out of 350 plus, were appearances on the NBC-TV "Today Show" and a radio interview with Dr. James Dobson on his "Focus on the Family."

For the "Today Show," our daughter Maureen accompanied me on the trip to New York. We were impressed with the first-class arrangements and the limo which picked us up for our ride to the NBC studio. Our daughter Tracy joined me for the California trip for the Dobson interview. During our trip west, Tracy coached me over and over again on how I should respond during the interview. When we finally began the show, Dr. Dobson asked Tracy a simple question and she stammered to find an answer. However, he told her not to worry, that they could edit that portion out, but after that she had new tolerance and empathy for me.

My hope is that this newly revised and updated edition will reach many more families and multiply the benefits accomplished by the first edition.

CHAPTER ONE

The Full Nest Syndrome:
a growing phenomenon

Without a family, man, alone in the world,
trembles with the cold
—Andre Malraux, French novelist
held prisoner during World War II

Before the 1930s, almost all of America's children left their parents' homes only when they got married, enrolled in college, or went into the military service. It was the unusual person who left home without having a specific reason for doing so. Starting in the 1930s, however, there began a surge of young people who, upon reaching age 18, were off and out of the house. They were seeking independence, searching for themselves, or just getting out of an uncomfortable home situation. Thirty years later, the '60s saw the climax of the practice of getting out of the parental home as quickly as possible. This was, after all, the decade of avowed independence from authority. Today, there is a major trend in our society toward the Full Nest Syndrome, in which young adult children remain or return home. This type of family living is on the increase.

Despite this growing phenomenon, some people criticize parents for allowing a grown child to live at home, creating a "Full Nest." They also criticize the adult children living at home for refusing to become "independent." But it seems short-sighted to criticize such an age-old custom.

In past centuries, in our own and in other cultures, it was common for family members, regardless of age, to live in one home—grandparents, parents and grandchildren. Generally, there was no magical time when an individual had to move from a parent's home in order to be recognized as an adult. Even today, in a few pocket geographical areas, the Old World style of several generations living under one roof has persisted as the norm.[2]

In our Western world, this multi-generational family is occurring once again—with a new twist. Now adult grown children, many of whom had left home, are returning to their parents' homes. At the time of the 1990 United States Census, a whopping 18 million adult offspring were living in their parents' home.[3]

When contemplating numbers of this magnitude, it's certainly appropriate for us to re-examine the phenomenon of more young people staying with their parents.

Today, the Full Nest Syndrome, as some parents term it, is causing quite a sociological stir as well as raising a number of questions. One assumption we can make is that, traditionally, there have been certain informal guidelines by which the family with adult offspring was ruled. But what are these guidelines? Have they been lost through the gap of the past 40 to 50 years, when few grown children lived at home? How many other families, besides yours and mine, are struggling by trial and error to make this recurring phenomenon work?

Kathryn, an acquaintance, related the following conversation that she overheard one day while shopping:

"Hi, Sally! Why, it must be six years since we've last talked. Your kids must be all grown and gone by now."

"Grown? Yes," replied Sally. "But gone? No! One is out of work, another is in college, a third is in a postgraduate program. And, then there's Molly. You know she's divorced and raising her little girl. They're both back home with us now, too, because she isn't getting

any child support from her ex-husband."

Many families with grown children living at home feel isolated, as if they were the only ones in this situation. But the conversation with Sally, simple as it is, is being repeated in varying ways by parents all over the country. Slowly, as the phenomenon increases, adult offspring living at home are "coming out of the closet" to discover there are millions of others in the same situation.

As the numbers of young people living at home increase, so do the numbers of parents who worry. They often are concerned that by allowing their grown kids to live at home, they'll be encouraging them to remain—stagnating forever in their birthplace. However, my research shows that most young people will leave the parental home as soon as they are financially and emotionally able to do so. Some may have to come back temporarily, one or more times, and it's only the exceptional individual who will stay on, and on and on. Almost all live-in adult young people are home temporarily, and not lifelong. In most cases, these offspring don't want to, or can't afford to, set up their own households because of inflation, high education costs, expensive rent and utility bills, unemployment or other economic reasons. Some may need emotional support following a separation, or divorce, or for job stress.

What are the parents' motives for allowing the Full Nest Syndrome to occur? "Having a good family life" tops the list of objectives that 96 percent of Americans have set for themselves, according to a Louis Harris survey of 1,220 adults nationwide.[4] This consensus indicates just how important the family is to most people.

But wanting, and having, are two different things. It takes a lot of hard work, determination, and caring to make a "good family life" come about, especially if one's family includes grown children living at home. There are often financial and emotional conflicts, with the result that family members may have to make concessions. However, unique benefits also exist for those who make the effort to look for them. "We've discovered that we appreciate many of the same things," writes the father of a 28-year-old son living at home. "I find that I enjoy his company, his wit, and his intelligence." He added, "When he leaves I'll probably regret it."[5]

In another family, the mother, a single parent, feels that it's less lonely, albeit more work and expense, with her three grown children (ages 30, 25 and 18 years) living at home.

What makes a child a child?

Children require a "warm, protected and prolonged period of nurture," one writer said.[6] But, historically, it took certain cultures a long time to recognize this need. Some periods in European history deemed the early years of a person's life so unimportant that the child was considered a non-person. Later, there was a period when children were mixed with adults "as soon as they were considered capable of doing without their mothers or nannies, not long after a tardy weaning at about the age of seven years."[7] The child was regarded as a small adult who mingled, competed, worked and played with mature adults.

The peoples of primitive eras and in ancient Greek times at least recognized a transition between the world of children and that of adults, which they celebrated by means of an initiation or an educational stage.[8] However, this important transitional stage was lost in time, and during the medieval centuries, life was either child's play or man's work.

The concept of childhood as a separate and important stage of development grew slowly over the centuries, but it was not until the beginning of the 15th century that the age of childhood was "discovered." In 1550, it was finally decided that there were three recognizable stages in a person's life: childhood, youth (which then meant the prime of life) and old age.[9]

During the 18th century, adolescence was recognized as a transition from childhood to adulthood, in part because formal education was introduced. It was when children started attending school that adults began to understand the various stages of childhood. As schooling became more formal and extended, age division became more acute. At this time, growing stages became defined as infancy, childhood, adolescence and young adulthood.

As the centuries rolled along, the period of being a child was extended, and these various stages of childhood emerged and crystallized. Many people came to believe that children needed a prolonged dependency on their parents to have a healthy, emotional development.[10]

However, this concern ceased abruptly when the child reached early adulthood. It seemed that when a child reached age 18 he or she had emerged automatically into adulthood and no longer required attention. One wonders why. We have now come to a time in history at which we should acknowledge one more stage of development—the time of transition from adolescence to the total self-supportive stage of competent adulthood. For many, this is an vital phase of development that needs to be recognized by society as a whole.

Upon reflection, it is quickly evident that there is no specific word for the grown child who lives at home. What should we call this person? "Child" won't do, for surely he or she isn't! "Offspring" is too awkward and is not a readily used or a common term. "Grown child" seems too clumsy.

We have a name for every other age group: embryo, fetus, infant, baby, toddler, pre-schooler, child, adolescent, teen, juvenile, or young person. And, then the term jumps to "adult." Most certainly, with the vast array of words in our language, we should have a label for over-18, transition-age young adults.

I suggest the term, "nester," by definition, "an adult offspring living in the parental home." This seems an appropriate definition of a young adult straddling youth and adulthood, with one foot in the world of dependency and the other taking searching steps into independency.

What is a family?

Originally, the word "family" meant "dweller in a household." According to *Webster*'s dictionary, family now means a "group of persons consisting of two parents and all their children." Today, many professionals enlarge the concept of family to mean a "group of persons living under the same roof, including both those actually related by blood, and all the others (dependents and friends), forming the household." For the purpose of this book, the meaning of family will be parents, children and others, regardless of age, related by blood or adoption living in the same household.

For a more in-depth description of the concept of "family" as relating to nesters, let's examine commonly accepted responsibilities. The family provides food, shelter, protection, and security, as well as emotional support to its members. According to columnist Ellen Goodman, "The family is formed not for the survival of the fittest, but for the weakest. It is not an economic unit, but an emotional one. This is not the place where people ruthlessly compete with each other, but where they work for each other. Its business is taking care, and when it works, it is not callous but kind.... We don't have to achieve to be accepted by our families. We just have to be. Our (family) membership is not based on credentials but on birth."[11]

Most offspring in the animal world are ready to live life apart from their parents at a relatively early age. Not so with human offspring. They require a period of growth, commonly considered to be 18 years, before they are ready to leave the nest and function apart from the family.

However, millions of grown children are finding that it takes longer than 18 years. And, in this world far from the simple life of farmer, baker, and cabinet-maker of pre-1900, some professionals even see the maturing process extending past age 30. Daniel Levinson, Ph.D., a pioneer in the study of adult development, feels that the whole process of entering adulthood lasts from about age 17 to age 33![12]

Nesters need to feel loved, encouraged and welcomed during this time of transition. Often the nesters leave and return, then leave again only to return once more. In many instances, the periods of time away from the parental home gradually become increasingly longer until the homecoming falls into a new category: a visit.

"The study of the family is in large part the study of how people have come to terms with the basic facts of life—not only with mating, child-bearing and child-rearing but with work and play, as well as with survival in a sometimes hostile environment and with the critical changes that come with aging and with death," according to one set of authors.[13]

Many of our nesters have certainly found life outside the parental home a "hostile environment."

To meet the particular needs of its members, families have devised all sorts of living arrangements, such as living together in one house, rural children living with city relatives, or separate apartment living away from the family for more established, older children. Families differ, though, because the needs of members differ. Some grown children are able to function on their own outside the family home, but others need more time with their parents. The family with nesters is a response to grown children who still want, or need, to live in the parental home.

The relationship between parents and their children is, for the most part, the closest, most intimate association people experience outside the marriage bond. Volumes have been written about the interaction between parents and their young children.

But today there is a need for more literature to cover the relationship between parents and their adult offspring. After all, we spend the greater part of our total lives as adults. Relating to each other as one adult to another adult is a totally different relationship than adult to child.

This new relationship brings both benefits and problems. As

one writer describes it: "In real life, living under one roof produces as much misery as joy, but a good deal of both."[14]

Another writer feels that if a family can work out its problems and enjoy the benefits of grown children living in the parental home, they will know an extra fullness to life. Sharing life with others gives us great happiness, and of course, our happiness is magnified when we can share our lives with those persons who are our own adult offspring.[15]

Family types

There are several ways of labeling families, but two categories that most sociologists agree on is the nuclear and the traditional family. *Roget's Thesaurus* gives the definition of nuclear as: "center, heart, core, kernel, basis or foundation." The nuclear family, therefore, generally consists of a husband, wife and their minor (under age 18) children. The traditional family consists of the nuclear group which will welcome other family members in need of a home.

The traditional family. Families of this type take in the young, the old and the needy. In this setting, an elderly grandparent, a homeless niece or a grown son or daughter is welcome anytime at home. This family is receptive, responsive, and resilient. It is especially open to the needs of its children, whatever their age. Because of their acceptance of kindred responsibilities and commitments, parents are willing for a time to set aside their own plans for the greater benefit of the whole family. They do this out of a sense of loyalty, feeling they want to share their home and lives with those who need or want to live with them. If one person is in need of special care and loving support, either on a short or a long-term basis, be it financial, emotional or physical, he or she is given all that the family can bestow.[16]

Certain needs can best, and sometimes only, be met by the immediate family. The self-oriented, individualistic, "I'm for me" attitude prevalent in our society, makes a traditional family seem exceptional in this day and age.

Scope of young adult nesters. Of the 18 million adult off-spring living in the parental home, the majority are the young, 18-to-24 year olds. Out of a total of 25 million, 13 million, or 53 percent are living in the parental home. This is over half of all young people in this age group!

Out of a total of 43 million 25 to 35 year olds, 5 million or 12 percent are living at home. The following charts show that the rate of increase of 18 to 24 year olds living with their parents is increasing at a much faster rate than the 25 to 34 year olds. Interestingly, males 25 to 34 years old are much more apt to live at home than females. A Census Bureau report states that the reason is generally because males marry later than females.

Young adults living with parents, 1960 - 1990

Source: U.S. Census Bureau

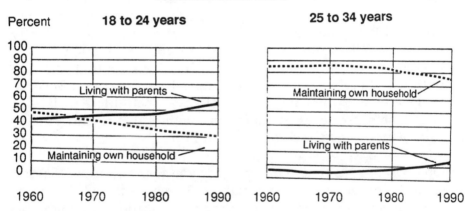

Changing relationships. In these changing times, millions of families are being asked to extend themselves a little further and for a longer period of time than some parents had original-ly intended. One mother (housing three offspring all in their 20s) rationalized sacrifice of time. "Statistics say I'll be living longer, so I guess I can make up this time, that I thought I'd have to myself, at a later date." Millions of families have risen to a similar challenge.

The John Kneebone family is a present-day traditional family. Mr. Kneebone, a 59-year-old grocer from Boulder, Colorado, says: "Five of our seven children, ages 15, 17, 23, 26 and 30, still live at home. The other two live nearby. We've always been a very close family. None of the kids has ever given us any real problems—like with drugs and alcohol. We've done things together since they were very young. The only hard thing now is getting everyone free from work at the same time so that we can take a vacation together." This family has discovered the secret of a happy family life.[17]

One woman reflected the attitude of a traditional family when she stated, "I feel that there is no age that you can shut the door and lock it, keeping out your grown children."

A mother of 10 children, with one grown child and five younger children living at home, related: "My relatives regard the home as a permanent living place until marriage, and are horrified if anyone suggests moving out before it is absolutely necessary. When our second child, a daughter, turned 18 and was going to move out, Grandmother insisted that she live with her, thereby continuing a 'family living' pattern. Surprisingly and happily, the 18-year-old was delighted to live at Grandma's house even under the watchful eye and curfew rules which were the same as at our home."

One parent said that she hopes her younger children, "having seen the older ones who remain at home, will feel that they, too, are welcome to stay when they reach adulthood, no matter what the current trends are toward moving out when they reach 18."

The nuclear family. Today, traditional family living seems to have gone out of vogue. In pursuit of better jobs, families are moving more often than in times past, further disrupting relations among family members. Distances between families are growing and family ties have weakened. Gradually, the smaller, nuclear family is replacing the traditional family, and children are growing up not knowing their cousins, aunts, uncles—and even, in some cases, their grandparents.

The nuclear family that has evolved in the more advanced and affluent Western societies characteristically takes a different view of its responsibilities. The goal is generally the greatest comfort of each of its members, and it tries to find a course of action that is best for all concerned. It frequently calls in outside professional advice, and often is eager to abdicate its caretaking function to outside authorities. Everybody goes out, or is taken out periodically, for treatment by doctors, dentists, orthodontists, psychiatrists and family consultants, and on their recommendation a family may pack off difficult or hopeless cases to institutions for periods ranging from a few hours to the remainder of a lifetime. In fact, the proliferation of kindergartens, day-care centers, hospitals, asylums and retirement homes is one of the characteristics that distinguishes modern Western society from all other societies past and present.

In such institutions, efficient, bureaucratic care replaced, or is supposed to replace, the generally affectionate and well-intentioned but perhaps slap-dash methods of relatives ministering to their kin in private dwellings. What the new method gains in efficiency, it may lose in the human warmth provided by an old-fashioned family in an old-fashioned home.[18]

The nuclear family faces isolation, having only two adults to share its burdens. Some historians feel that the nuclear family is now in a further state of transition and decay, since even the family members are becoming isolated from each other. They spend little time with each other because both parents work outside the home and the children spend their hours in day-care centers or schools.

Fathers, who once held authority and were seen as the family's pillar of strength, now stand in want of some respect from their own children. Family ties, which were once strong, now are weak with lack of communication between even the immediate members of some families. Perhaps the constant mobility of families is a factor in this isolation that so many people are experiencing.

To nest or not, that is the question

In some families, no home is big enough to house two generations, for lack of room or tolerance. The young are exhorted to go to college, go west—in short, to get out.[19] Sometimes, these feelings are right out front, but often they are submerged deep in the subconscious and are difficult to admit. One father on the Phil Donahue Show was finally able to verbalize his feelings:

"I feel the parents' responsibility is to make sure your kids are edu-cated. Make sure that if they have a problem, or really have trouble, that they are able to come home. But at the time their education is finished, my kids understand they're moving out. I don't think two families can live together," the father stated.

"Once they get the baccalaureate," Phil started to question, "once they graduate..."

The father interrupted, "...they're on their own!"

"Write them off the hook?"

"Yeah," the father responded. "Once they move out of my house, from under my control, they're cut off. And they know it."

"It's clear that you've come a long way without my advice; but just for the sake of our conversation," said Phil, "I sense in you and in lots of other men around the country an authoritarian attitude, which says, 'This is the way it is and this is my house.' Is this the kind of attitude that opens dialogue, understanding, friendship and caring between fathers and sons, mothers and daughters, parents and kids? If we are sustaining real pain in many households across the country because of people who don't share feelings, is it possible that this judgmental attitude is at the bottom of this inability to com-municate?"

"I have had a little difficulty communicating with my daughter, in fact," admitted the father.[20]

This father may just have realized that his lack of communication may well have been one of the contributing causes of his unyielding attitude toward his children. Phil concluded that in our present culture there seems to be a prevailing negative attitude toward intimate relationships which carry responsibilities. "It looks like we can't wait to get rid of each other," he said. "We can't wait to get separated."[21]

Actually, there seems to be no set rule about whether it's best for adult offspring to live with their parents. One adult offspring said: "I don't feel it's a question of what you should do or what you shouldn't do (nesting or not). It's what's right for you and your parents. Personally, I don't agree with the idea of living at home at the age of 30. But, you know, for some it's okay."[22]

The decision of whether an adult offspring should nest or not depends a lot on the current capabilities of the parent. Violet Arnold, a Minneapolis psychotherapist, remembers when her grown daughter telephoned to say she wanted to move home—again. She had been in and out many times previously.

This time, however, Violet felt that she would not be able to tolerate a return move. So she told her daughter, "Let's have lunch together and talk about it." Violet felt that they wouldn't be able to get too emotional in a public place. Over a bowl of soup, she told her daughter: "I love you very, very much, but I am not, at this time, able to handle your moving back home."

Fortunately, tears were spared and understanding reigned. The daughter accepted her mother's statement and said she still loved her mom anyway. In turn, Violet found other ways to give her daughter the emotional support she wanted and needed.

Certainly, not all adult children should or do live at home. Some grown children don't need to nest. They have managed to become independent and have no desire to live with or to receive financial support from their parents. Not every family is able to house all its grown children who need a home. These parents may not have the finances, space or stamina to allow their grown children to live at home.

"I believe having an adult offspring in the home is a good thing when the relationship is productive, tension-free and happy," writes one nester, "but if this isn't possible, if things can't be worked out, it's best to separate."

Another young adult puts it a little stronger: "I do not live at home and I would not live at home. I pretty much had my freedom when at home, but I didn't like it. My mother and I just drove each other crazy!"

Children would rather move out if the home situation is not ideal—when, for example, one of the parents is an alcoholic, or when there is a case of intense friction between the parents themselves.

Sadly, sometimes home is just too painful a place to live, and it's best to leave. One woman with an alcoholic husband wrote that all of their children left home immediately after graduating from high school.

Some grown children who move outside the parental home still need help to be able to live well—usually in the form of regular or occasional financial assistance.

One mother related, "Christie (her grown daughter living in an apartment) has been unemployed for three months. Never once did she ask to come back home, because she was striving for independence. She did, however, ask me to pay a utility bill for her, which I did." Some parents who are unable to accommodate their adult offspring in their home choose instead to help them with loans or gifts of money.

One mother felt there should be a limit to the time a grown offspring lived at home. "While I would want a 25-year-old to be out on his own," wrote one mother, "I'd like to see an 18-year-old stay at home for another few years." This mother had three nesters, ages 25, 20 and 18.

Toward the Full Nest Family

Today, we have a growing phenomenon in our society—the Full Nest Family.

Between 1960 and 1990, the proportion of persons 18 to 24 years old who lived in the home of their parents increased from 43 percent to 53 percent. Among 25 to 34 year olds the figure also increased from 9 percent in 1960 to 12 percent in 1990. Society is being confronted with the need to take the Full Nest Family seriously.

Historians recognize two types of families—traditional and nuclear. It is the former who are more apt to house a nester. Many of these families are looking for constructive guidance to help them because, although this phenomenon of extended family living was common in past times, it is still unusual in our lifetime.

CHAPTER TWO

Lessons from nesters in past centuries and other cultures

*"Early departure from the homestead is a moral crisis
that many of our youth do not show themselves
able to meet. It comes at a tender age,
when Judgment is weakest
and passion and impulse strongest."*
—An anonymous 18th-century advocate
of keeping children at home longer than was customary.[1]

A glance into former times shows many examples of extended family living. Through the centuries, families have had adult members remaining at home. At times, this was the result of grown children who didn't want, or were unable, to set up their own households. In a few cultures, children were traditionally bound to live in the parental home. When seen in historical perspective, we can view living-in as customary and ordinary. Peter Laslett, social historian, says it well when he calls this "understanding ourselves in time," for understanding history is the key to understanding the present.[2]

Extended households in Europe. Extended family living was common in Europe, from the earliest centuries until the Industrial Revolution. There was not much privacy since households usually included a lot of people—grandparents,

parents and children—in a small area. This was intense family living to its fullest: food, slumber and recreation had to be shared in common. All family members had no choice but to participate in the fine art of sharing, as do full nest families in our day.

The reasons behind multi-generational family living was much the same as today—economic recession, the burden of taxation and its method of assessment. There was also one added element: depopulation. As an aftermath of the Black Death or plague, many of the breadwinners in the families had died, leaving families destitute and forced to live together. Often the grandfather and his eldest son worked the family farm. Subsequent sons either stayed single and remained on the family farm, or were "paid a sum of money (as their inheritance) by the eldest son to go off on their own."[3]

Extended living is common in some countries, even in comparatively recent times. In a 1956 survey of 10,000 rural homes in 23 communities in Serbia, 26 percent were extended families, with some communities having as many as 55 percent and even 62 percent extended family homes.

Historian Laslett states that persons living in such close relationships with others eventually developed an ability for "intense communication" both among themselves, and with their communities. Thus, one can easily suppose that living together like this would develop an intimate relationship among family members.

Poverty in the European countries. In 18th century Holland, custom dictated that people could marry only when they were able to support a family. Those who couldn't afford this luxury stayed single and lived out their lives in their parents' homes. In many cases, if a family had more than one son, only one was able to get married and he wasn't able to do so until he was older. Unmarried daughters also stayed on in the family home.[4]

So the extended household evolved. In the Netherlands

province of Overijssel, there were 7,763 households in the year 1749, and 20.5 percent were extended family homes. The percentage was a bit higher in the rural areas (22.6 percent) than it was in the villages (15.3 percent).[5]

Even in more recent times, in the eastern part of the Netherlands during the early 1950s, 25 percent of farms were being worked by a family living with one of the married partner's parents.[6] It is still common for Dutch offspring to live at home until they are finished with their education, at about the age of 25.

In 19th century Serbia, the population was multiplying, and land began to fill up. Economic and social competition developed since mass migration still hadn't occurred in this country, as it had elsewhere throughout Europe. The multigenerational household flourished. In many families, several married sons joined together with their fathers in living and working together. After the father's death, several brothers and their families continued to live on in the same home.

In parts of Yugoslavia today, farm households are extremely large. The limited availability of land or other economic opportunity, combined with a normal increase in population, continues to enlarge the size of individual modern farm households, for the children still have nowhere else to go.[7] Some current households are remarkably large. For example, the household of Bajram Bujari contained 60 persons in 1958, with everyone (except the spouses) being descendants of Bajram's own grandfather. This type of family living requires a parental head with a respected authority, to ensure the smooth functioning of the household.[8]

The extended families were in a good position to multiply their property and become economically secure, because of their manpower.[9] Even so, when economic conditions are kinder and money is more readily available, people seem to prefer to live separately in small family units,[10] but usually still in close geographical location.

Today, as in the past, many people are feeling the financial pinch, especially young people. Many grown children can't afford to live away from the family home. Our tolerance for the nester, therefore, should be based on historical perspective. It has been done before!

Sexual maturity and marriage age in Europe and America. One of the perplexing problems of the nester today is the ever-widening gap between sexual maturity and marriage. Studies of the last 100 years indicate that children are maturing at an increasingly earlier age, while at the same time young adults are marrying later and later. Some countries have long kept extensive records of the age of onset of menstruation. Thus we know that our children are maturing sooner as time goes on. The table, *Maturation Ages*, shows the decrease in the average age of onset of menstruation.[11]

MATURATION AGES

Country	Maturation age then	Maturation age now
Norway	1850: 17.1 years	1951: 13.5 years
Sweden	1905: 15.7 years	1949: 14.1 years
U.S.	1904: 14.1 years	1991: 12.5 years[12]

The above figures are *median ages* only. This means that as many girls began menstruation before these dates as after. Some reach the onset of menstruation as early as 8 or 9 years. Others mature later, with 17 being considered within the norm.

The exception to the above norms of maturation were the children of the elite in 19th century Europe. They matured at an earlier rate than the children of the poor. This meant greater physical achievement at an earlier age for the wealthy, giving them yet another advantage over the poor.

There was a difference of 3.5 inches in height and 11.5 pounds in weight between the poorest working class boys and the better off working class boys in York, England, in 1899. "The privileged, wealthy children must have been taller, heavier, better developed and earlier to mature than the rest;

the males must have had beards and broken voices much sooner, the women must have become full women much more quickly."[13]

So the children of the rich matured sooner and gained physical strength sooner than did the children of the poor. But the average overall ages of sexual maturation in 19th century Europe were about 3.5 years later than present day figures.

The picture emerges of children becoming sexually mature earlier than their parents did, but having to wait a longer period before marriage. Current social, educational and economic problems are forcing our young people to marry later, causing another social problem: that of sexually active, unmarried young adults. Because they are marrying later, many of these young people are living in the parental home.

Over the centuries, the age at which young people customarily married has fluctuated. The later they married, the longer single children stayed at home with their parents. There were many reasons for people marrying later. The Medieval English, 19th century Americans, and Irish of all generations give us striking examples.

Most young people of Medieval England waited until their middle 20s before considering marriage. This is exceptionally late when we consider these people had a life expectancy of 48, once they reached adulthood.[14]

When Medieval English young men reached marriage age, they were unable to wed until they had a nest egg to launch their new family. "When a son got married he left the family of his parents and started a family of his own," writes Laslett about Medieval England. "If he was not in a good financial position to do this, then he could not get married, nor could his sister unless the man who was to take her for his bride was in a position to start a new family."[15] A few wealthy Medieval English young women married at an early age, between 13 and 15 years, for they matured early and had the financial means to wed. It is interesting to note that in the play "Romeo and

Juliet," Shakespeare convincingly put Juliet's age at 14, for she was one of the privileged wealthy class.

Traditionally, there were a lot of curtailments pertaining to marriage. For example, throughout the generations, even until today, the traditional family in Ireland stays together for a long time. Upon his marriage, a son is entitled to a property settlement. If there is no property to inherit, he may have to stay single until he accumulates some means to support a wife and family. This can take decades, and in some cases the money is never accumulated, thus making him ineligible for marriage.

Lack of hard cash in farming families makes it difficult or even impossible for fathers to pay sons a salary on the family farm. If the son is to inherit the estate from his father, he will generally have to wait until his father is good and ready to retire and hand it over. When the father feels it is time, he and his wife move into a smaller bedroom and the son and his wife take the main bedroom, along with the title to the farm. It sometimes happens that the son has to wait so long that he becomes a confirmed bachelor and loses the inclination to marry.[16] Younger sons, knowing that the inheritance will go to the eldest, often leave the family farm and migrate to the city for employment.

Family affection in 19th century America. Throughout the years, it was affection among family members which kept some nesters at home. Parents and children enjoyed each other and wanted to live together. Lasch and Taylor wrote that the American family in the 1840s lost its economic function (because people no longer grew their own food), and their educational function (because schools taught their children.)[17] So the families that remained together did so no longer out of need, but out of affection.

Thomas Jefferson, widowed early, felt that he was an absentee father throughout his political career. He tried through letters to guide his motherless daughters. Upon his retirement, he moved back to his home in Monticello, and his daughter, Martha, and her family moved there, as they always did when the president returned from Washington. Martha was her father's companion during his later years. It was certainly affection that held this family together and made their life meaningful.[18]

Like the Jeffersons, and countless other families throughout the ages, many nesters in our day live in the parental home because they want to, saying that it's a happy, loving period that they and other family members enjoy.

Dictatorial parents in the Iroquois Indian tribes and ancient Rome. Nesters who feel that they have little freedom because of an authoritarian or dictatorial parent may find comfort in taking a look at former customs of Iroquois Indians. "When an Iroquois mother felt that her son was ready to marry, somewhere around the age of 22, she sought out a young woman who she thought he might like. The two mothers met and arranged a wedding date. Often the two young people didn't know about the marriage until a day or two before the wedding. It would have been considered disrespectful for the young couple to protest their mothers' decision."[19] Some nesters today complain of parents who are interfering, but few parents today go to this extent.

Today's nesters who chafe at their authoritarian parents might feel less irritated if they delved into history and discovered the "Papa Power" of ancient Rome. The father had complete control over his children and his son's children. After birth, the infant was placed at his father's feet. If he picked the baby up, the child became part of the family. If he did not, this meant total rejection. The baby was left by the side of the road to die or to be taken away by a stranger, perhaps as a slave.

Even after a son was grown and married, his father controlled his money and his property. The father could arrange for his children to divorce, with or without their consent. His authority was so far-reaching that if he thought he had cause, he could even sell his son. However, this was hardly ever done. His power over his children extended even to death, for he had the authority, vested in him by government, after conferring with other family members, to condemn any of his children to death. He rarely did this though, as it was frowned upon by society.[20]

To be sure, some of our current nesters feel that they have a dictatorial or authoritarian parent, but seen in comparison to ancient Rome, our nesters' situations may look rather mild.

Married nesters in China and the Maya Indian tribes. Down through history, we have examples of married children living in the parental home. Some countries had strong traditions which dictated how and where the newly married couple would live.

In China, the son was the nester, for he remained at home even after marrying, bringing his bride into his parents' home. Through long-standing custom, the new bride was chosen by her husband from a different village or part of the city. She then lived in her husband's parents' household, which was dominated by the fierce figure of her mother-in-law. Customarily, the mother-in-law humiliated the new bride—a tradition which was handed down from generation to generation, breeding misery and resentment. Each bride, in turn, repeated the cycle when she became a mother-in-law. Pressures became so intense that the suicide rate among females in the 21-to-30 age group was 31 times as great as it was among males.[21]

The new bride had to be totally subservient to her husband, father-in-law and mother-in-law. She was forced to be obedient and affectionate. In addition, her role as daughter-in-law took precedence over her role as wife.

Things got a little better when another son married and brought home a wife. The first wife then had seniority and status, and the new wife was at the bottom of the totem pole. Matters did not improve noticeably even when the mother-in-law died, for then the wife of the eldest son was the first woman of the house and could force the wives of other sons to do her bidding.[22]

When Geraldine Rhoads, editor of *Women's Day* magazine,

was traveling in China in 1980, she found that the editors of a comparable women's magazine in China still considered one of the more common personal problems to be mothers-in-law. She wrote that it was still customary for a Chinese bride to live with her husband's family. Their houses and apartments are tiny by our standards, and close quarters certainly created even more friction. Grandparents minded the children while mothers and fathers worked during the day.[23]

The Mayans of the 10th century in Central America also accommodated the newly married couple in the parental home. This society was matrilocal, meaning that newly married couples lived in the bride's family home, but only on a temporary basis of five years. The new groom was expected to present a gift to this father-in-law, live in his home and work for him during those years. This time may well have been used to acquire knowledge for later independent living. After the five compulsory years in the bride's parental home, the entire community celebrated by joining together and building a new house for the young couple.[24]

There are indications that married children and their families are returning to the parental home in ever-increasing numbers in our day. One real-estate agent reports that she is now seeing at least one family grouping (family plus married child with family) per week that wants to buy a home together. Many of these present-day joint householders find that if they work out details in advance regarding chores, finances, and a projected date when the married nesters plan to move, this can be a time of economic and emotional growth.

Single parent nesters in Japan through the 13th century. With an ever-increasing rate of single parents in our present day, it is understandable that a certain percentage do live in the parental home. For them, it might be interesting to be aware of a cultural tradition on this subject in another country.

Customs in Japan differed from other cultures in that, up until the 14th century, a Japanese wife remained with her own family. Her husband visited her only by night. He did not live with her. The Japanese word for marriage meant "to slip by night into the house"! So, for that period in Japanese history, through the 13th century, the daughter was a nester and she lived in her parents' home, raising her children without the daily support or company of a husband or a father for her children.[25] The grandparents, though, were able to support the wife and give guidance to the grandchildren.

The situation of a Japanese wife in many ways is very similar to our present-day, single-parent nester in that she raises her children without the help of the father.

Because of soaring land costs, many young Japanese now find it impossible to buy a house of their own. As one reporter stated, "Think you pay too much for housing? Be thankful you don't live in Japan, where small houses an hour's commute from Tokyo start at $500,000. In the city they go for more than $1 million. Since few can afford these prices, Japanese banks have begun offering 100-year mortgages to be paid by the borrower's children."[26]

Family affluence in the Trobriand Islands. Life was easy for the Trobrianders, a group of people living in the southwest corner of the Pacific Ocean. They made their living with a minimum of effort by harvesting yams out of the jungle and reaping the vast benefits of the sea. The Trobriand children formed a body, a group apart, separate from the adults, much like our young teenagers. Often this group of young people were in opposition to their parents. They "led a happy, free, Arcadian existence, devoted to amusement and the pursuit of pleasure."[27]

They were not expected to do any work and so they didn't. This hardly prepared them for the adult responsibilities of caring for a family. However, Trobriand parents discovered that eventually their children did settle down into stable family life, just as their parents did before them.

Paul Kingsley, a California psychiatrist, feels that we may not be helping our young people assume adult responsibility as well as we could. Our offspring grow up not knowing what is expected of them, he says, and thus are unprepared to accept adult responsibility.

Some children turn 18 and are told, "You are now legally an adult." They are then pushed out into life without much preparation.[28] However, even with this lack of direction at age 18, almost all offspring do generally follow in their parents' lifestyle sooner or later.

Commonality of nesting

Through the perspective of a brief historical and cultural scan, it becomes apparent that nesting is not unusual. Extended family living was, and still is, common in many cultures—as it has been for centuries. Poverty, a later marrying age, affection, or a need for emotional support are all reasons why grown children have remained in the parental home.

Certainly, these same reasons apply with equal validity today. Factors such as a dictatorial parent can make remaining at home a difficult situation. However, there are many benefits in extended family living, such as the opportunity to save money and to maintain a close family bond.

Viewed in historical perspective, we can see that nesting can be considered common, ordinary and useful. Indeed, understanding the history of adult children living at home really is the key to understanding today's Full Nest Family.

CHAPTER THREE

Reasons for nesting

"Where there is room in the heart
there is always room in the house."
— St. Thomas More, a 15th century author,
statesman, and scholar who was a devoted family man.[1]

L et's examine the major reasons why grown sons and daughters live in the parental home. Some are nesting out of their own desire—they feel that Mom and Dad's place is where they want to live. Others remain home out of need—financial, emotional and social. By analyzing nesters' many motives, your family may see some parallels that will help you understand your own situation more fully.

The desire to nest

S ome nesters are in the parental home out of desire—they just want to live there. These nesters, and their families, see many benefits to living together.

"Our adult children are living at home because that is where they like to live, and we love to have them," writes one mother with three adult offspring and several younger children at home. "We have built many memories together. My husband and I hear the joy and laughter of our children ring throughout the house and feel we are truly blest."

One 31-year-old nester writes that she enjoys the physical comforts of living at home. She also appreciates the parental love and friendship, and the monetary savings. She writes, "We have a mutually respectful adult relationship with each other." She does qualify her remarks by saying, "But if the situation were not good at home, I would adjust my finances and live elsewhere."

One day while hunting, a 24-year-old nester and his dad had an opportunity to talk. The son told his dad how tough it was getting used to the factory line, how wrenching it was to see so many of his friends move away or get married. Dad confided to his son that he sometimes still felt inadequate at his job even after 20 years at the plant. As father and son talked, they found they agreed on the joys of hunting and fishing, but that they disagreed on gyros and jazz. Suddenly, they realized that their conversation sounded like two ordinary people just chatting. When had their father/son relationship turned the corner from parent and child to being friends? Living at home had cemented the relationship.

A *New York Times* report points out that some families with married children living at home experience a "warmer sense of belonging and closeness at a time of widespread personal alienation."[2] Living together seems to foster feelings of loyalty by strengthening the ties that bind.

A 23-year-old Army veteran says that he can't find any good reason for leaving home. "My home town area is great and my family is full of love." He relishes his mother's home cooking. He appreciates the laundry that is neatly folded. Not having the burden and expense of maintaining his own household is extremely attractive to him.

"Apartment living would be lonely," writes a 19-year-old female living at home. Also living in the family home besides her parents, are two adult sisters, as well as two younger siblings. "I feel that living together enriches the family unit and makes for a happy, cheerful home life. We're just not ready to leave the family home yet."

One mother of three nesters feels that her young adults support each other. She relates that two of her nesters like to keep an eye on their 21-year-old sister, who is sometimes rebellious, and occasionally abuses drugs and alcohol.

Some nesters are living at home partly because of the protection it offers from overzealous suitors. One female nester feels that, because she lives at home, it is easier to "just say no." The implied feeling that a boyfriend may encounter her father tends to dampen a young man's ardor. But young women are not the only ones who appreciate this protection. Some male nesters also like shelter from overzealous companions. One 32-year-old bachelor was especially dismayed at the forward actions of various female friends who came to visit him in his apartment. He said this never happens now that he lives at home again.

Nesting out of financial need

One of the most common reasons that nesters said they lived at home was economic:

"I can't afford to live outside the parental home."
"I was laid off from my job."
"I do not want to experience a drop in my scale of living."
"Home is nicer than any apartment that I could afford to rent."
"I'm looking for a job."
"When living at home, I have fewer bills to worry about."

Almost all nesters say that at least one of their reasons for nesting is economic hardship. This makes reduced living costs one of the most important advantages to living at home. The old saying is, "Two can live as cheaply as one." Well, it follows that three can live just about as cheaply as two—or almost. It's certainly true that adding one more person to a household isn't nearly as expensive as one person living singly and paying the bills alone.

Many young people are finding it increasingly difficult to be financially independent. They really need and appreciate the assistance of their parents: minimal or free room and board, and/or periodic loans or gifts.

Nesting to save money

Even though 90 percent of the nesters stated that they are living at home because of economic hardship, 51 percent reported that while living at home they were saving money. Many had goals that they were striving to achieve.

Saving is a good habit to cultivate and one that most Americans haven't seemed to acquire. Records show that, on the average, Americans have saved less than $700 per person.

By comparison, according to the International Savings Bank Institute in Geneva, Japanese per capita savings in 1990 were $45,118.[3] We can learn from other cultures that it's a great feeling to have a financial cushion in case the automobile's transmission and one's job fail in the same month.

It's generally cheaper for a young adult to live at home, even if he or she is paying room and board, since few nesters pay a sum equal to what it would cost them to live in an apartment or in a home of their own. This often helps the nester save money for some specific purpose: a car, clothes, college tuition, vacation, marriage or a down payment on a house.

Several nesters mentioned saving for a trip to Europe or other travels. One nester is investing in art equipment, saying that he "wants time to pursue his creative interests without the responsibility of independent living."

Another nester, a 25-year-old male, is investing in real estate and stock. He borrowed $7,000 from his parents, which he is paying back in monthly installments, along with his room-and-board payments of $120 a month.

Parents might also point out special savings that have tax advantages, i.e. 401Ks, IRAs, payroll deductions for U.S. savings bonds and employee stock option plans. A savings of 10 to 15 percent of income is recommended.

Forming adult relationships with parents

A stable, loving family relationship, on an adult-to-adult level, provides support, permanence and a strong foundation for daily living. A decided advantage of nesting is that parents and offspring have the opportunity to build a relationship as one adult to another. Most family members will spend the greater part of their lives relating to each other as adults. A quicker relationship transition can occur if they can work on this change on a daily basis.

One writer on the subject says, "If you can establish a mutually respectful relationship with your parents, you could, by staying on in the parental home, create a happy period when you and your parents can enjoy one another as adults."[4]

Nesters and their parents need to discuss duties for which each will be responsible when the child becomes an adult, whether after high school graduation or 18th birthday. If this is a return move home, this discussion should take place before the move happens, preferably at a neutral location. It may not be easy to set down responsibilities, but if a successful discussion does take place, everyone will be able to enjoy the nesting period to a far greater degree. They will be starting from a common base of understanding of expectations.

Often the burden of responsibility weighs heavily upon parents as they struggle to do the "right" things in raising their children. In our preoccupation with parental duties, we tend to overlook or miss some of the rewarding aspects of parenthood. We become too busy to stop and smell the flowers as we rush from chore to chore. As the years roll on, we realize that it's too late to do any significant changing or further training of our offspring. Instead, it's time to enjoy the results of our many years' labor.

For some parents, it comes as a surprise that they can enjoy their adult children as individuals. They're delighted to find that they have much in common. Then, when a word or a glance from their grown son or daughter triggers memories of days gone by, they often experience a warm glow of remembrance and a spontaneous chuckle. They find that now they can laugh together at yesterday's serious incident.

Nesting for companionship

Living together as a family provides many companionship advantages for parents and nesters. In addition, there can be particular advantages for the parent in situations of a death of a marriage partner, a divorce, or in growing old.

One mother writes, "We especially like to have another adult besides us parents living at home because we can go out and feel safe about the younger children. Then, too, when my husband recently went on a fishing trip, I was glad to have Al, our 28-year-old, living here. I felt safe and not lonesome. During the six years that Al has lived at home as an adult, my husband sometimes worked nights and I was glad to have another adult in the house. Moreover, I really value the use of his car. He arranges to leave it for me whenever I need it."

A 25-year-old male nester relates that, after his father died, his mother needed help in raising the three younger children. He moved back home, and his mother appreciated the support of an older male figure around the house.

One 26-year-old female nester, who moved home with her mother after her parents' divorce, now is able to offer emotional and financial support for the remaining large family. Her $175 monthly room-and-board payment augments her mother's income. "Rent is so steep," writes the nester, "that I don't want to be wasting my money by living alone in an apartment. I'd rather help to support the family at home."

In addition to the financial advantages for her, she loves the activity surrounding the family home. She claims she was lonely living in an apartment. Since it was cheaper for her to live at home, she was also able to start a savings account for a trip abroad.

Some elderly parents need assistance in daily chores. A nester who can help with the cooking, laundry, and shopping is a valuable asset in this special time of need. The nester can also be a companion to a parent who would otherwise be alone.

Nesters, as well as their parents, share the same advantages of companionship, especially in cases of illness or handicap, a traveling spouse, or a return from military service. There is an obvious advantage to living at home in these cases. The family is able to help this special nester with everyday living needs. With a disabled nester it is important that, as much as possible, the person with a handicap be allowed and encouraged to be a contributing part of the family.

Sometimes there are two nesters and more: a married off-spring, spouse or a child. Nesting helps them save money. Furthermore, when one of the partners has to do a lot of traveling, or is required to work late hours, the spouse left at home appreciates the companionship of the family. And working spouses know that even though they are not able to keep their mate company as much as they would like, the family can fill in.

One female nester is married to a Navy man, who is sometimes gone for months at a time. She says, "I have no other appropriate person with whom to live. My husband is gone so long, that apartment living would just be too lonely!" Instead, by living with her parents, she can experience everyday companionship and a family spirit that is joyous, loving and generous—one which binds that family together.

One woman told about the family in which the father lost his job and was unable to meet the mortgage payment. Unwilling to lose their home, and after much discussion with all family members concerned, this father, along with his wife and two children and pet dog, moved in with his wife's family. He then rented out his home. With this rental income he was able to meet the monthly mortgage payment. Creative financial maneuvering and accommodating in-laws are helping this family prevent the home loss during joblessness.

To house married nesters, some families are converting their homes into duplexes. They are creating separate residences in a basement, attic, or garage or adding an extension. This living arrangement can help the young couple accumulate a nest egg so that they can afford to move out later. When that happens, parents find that they can rent out these accommodations to provide extra funds upon retirement. Sometimes this extra space can be used as housing for an elderly parent.

Many returning veterans nest for a period of time. This is especially needed if the vet is physically or emotionally injured. This nester requires the loving support of family to help return to the life he or she had before, or to begin another one. John, one veteran who moved back home, responded to a call-in talk show. He said that he had developed a drug and alcohol addiction while in the service and was happy to move into the safety of his parents' home. "It was good to know," he said, "that my folks were there to welcome, accept and help me. This meant so much to me!"[5]

Nesting in order to mend relationships

Often, a child's adolescent years are emotionally difficult to parents and child. Things are said and incidents happen that cause deep hurts. However, living together as adults could be a good time to start healing wounds and rebuilding relationships.

A father and his teenage son, the fourth of their 10 children, were continually at odds. The son liked to party late, ignoring his father's curfew. Dad felt he had to stand firm or else he'd lose control, not only over that son, but all the remaining children. Home life became so difficult that during his senior year of high school, the son moved out of the parental home and lived in a tent in a friend's backyard. That school year, the friend's parents fed him and allowed him to use their bathroom and laundry facilities.

After he earned his high school diploma, he found work and rented an apartment. He married, but then divorced. Throughout the next eight years, he moved back in with his folks on several occasions—once for a short time before marriage, another time when he and his wife were having marital difficulties, and then again after the divorce. But each time, soon after he returned home, the fighting erupted again between son and father. His mother was at her wit's end, wondering how the difficulties could be resolved. Time after time, the parents would welcome him back, and time after time, the same old antagonisms would recur. Tragically, his dad was diagnosed with a fatal illness; he lingered for six months. One day when the son visited his dad in the hospital, they talked over their disagreements, mutually apologized and made their peace. Mercifully, the dad died two days later, leaving his son healed of a lifetime of bitter feuding.

Possibly if they had been able to resolve their differences earlier, the son wouldn't have needed to keep returning after he was an adult. Maybe his marriage would not have suffered, either, if he hadn't been so concerned with his father/son problem.

Some adult children also keep returning to the parental home, hoping to heal a troubled relationship with a parent. As long as hope lives, adult children will keep returning in an effort to right a wronged kinship.

After returning to live with her parents, one nester writes, "I have since absolved my guilty feelings of the terror I was to my parents as an adolescent. There was tremendous turmoil between myself and my parents, and between my parents themselves. Returning home brought our differences into the open. We also realized our true wishes to learn to accept each other for what we are." This family was able, during the nesting period, to talk over and resolve their difficulties. Returning home was a start in building their adult-to-adult relationship.

One mother writes that her 22-year-old daughter is loving to her younger siblings, but that she lacks confidence in herself. The mother attributes this to an unfortunate experience in the daughter's early years, when the child's grandfather lived in his daughter's home. At that time, the grandmother was in the hospital for a prolonged period. Because the mother shuttled back and forth to the hospital to visit the grandmother, and then spent extra time caring for the grandfather, it took too much attention away from the baby. The mother feels that her daughter had been short-changed at that time, and she is dedicated to giving her all the love she can now to make up for that lost time.

Some parents are providing rehabilitation for their nesters. One mother of a 21-year-old man working only part-time and not attending school writes, "He's trying to save money to go back to college and pay off debts incurred by trouble with the law and, we suspect, drugs. He struggled in college for two nine-month terms, but finally gave up. However, I feel that the Lord sent him back home now to us and our kinship. This is a time to rebuild his self-esteem."

One mother of a large family relates how, having her son, age 21, back home has affected their relationship. "He is able to get jobs, but gets laid off shortly after being hired. He couldn't afford to live elsewhere because he had loans to pay off, due to high-risk auto insurance payments. He says he came back home because he couldn't afford to get an apartment, but I've since come to realize that perhaps there was a subconscious reason in returning home—to repair damaged family feelings. Our improved relationship has come about gradually, as he gained inner strength against the pressures of society." She reports that they are now better able to enjoy each other's company as adults.

"The coming-home trend might just prove healthy," writes Ann, mother of nester Suzanna. "It's a step forward, because in order to get along in the world, it helps if you get along with your parents—even if they are difficult."[6]

Needing a haven

When out of a job. Some young people don't realize they need a sufficient, regular income to support themselves. Many rely upon their parents for money, and they don't feel that a permanent job is really desirable or even necessary.

One mother of a 24-year-old nesting daughter lamented, "Janie is unenthusiastic about working, and is unable to support herself. She has a difficult time getting and keeping a job because she has trouble taking orders." This same mother wonders, "It seems as if some of us allow our children to live at home because we think we are helping them in time of need. Could we be doing the opposite?"

L iving at home after becoming an adult can be either helpful or hurtful, depending on how the situation is handled. If the young adult continues to grow and mature while living in the parental home it is a helpful circumstance. By continuing to live on at home, the nester is usually forced to deal with other family members and to sharpen his or her ability to relate with others. A person living alone in an apartment has only himself or herself to be concerned about and can become selfish. Being forced to relate to others in a family living situation can be a growing experience. If, however, growth stops or if regression takes place, obviously that's not a healthy situation.

From the nester's point of view, the home as a financial haven can be seen differently. One young lady on the Donahue Show complained, "I think we're putting too much emphasis on the aspect of money."

Phil retorted, "What do you mean, too much emphasis? If you can't get a job, what are you going to do? We sent our children to college. They chose to major in Renaissance Literature and then they can't find a job. Now they're coming back home. I don't mean to make fun of those folks who are majoring in literature. Perhaps we could use more folks who care about the arts, letters, and culture. But the truth of the matter is, that it's a lot harder to find a job today than it was when I graduated."[7]

As Donahue indicated, perhaps our offspring need more guidance choosing a major in college, so that they have a marketable skill which will bring them a living wage after graduation. Then, perhaps our college graduates will be able to support themselves and won't be forced to nest penniless in parental homes.

Another nester carried her financial nonchalance even further. Tammy works only part-time and can't afford an apartment. "Tammy," her mother writes, "finds work too much of an effort and boring after the first few days." She's not paying room and board, because her parents don't need it. The little money that she makes working part-time is spent on clothes and wouldn't make any difference to her parents' finances even if it was paid to them as room and board. But quite possibly it would make a difference in Tammy's attitude toward work if she was required to pay room and board. Since these parents don't need room and board, in order to develop Tammy's sense of financial responsibility, they could require a weekly sum and then secretly save it for her eventual move from home. This would force her to become more industrious. Tammy's case illustrates that there can be fine line between pampering and helping a nester.

When a young person is nesting because he or she is out of work, the nester really does need a place to stay, food to eat, and, especially, encouragement. The family should have love and compassion for the nester at this time. Occasionally when nesters are out of work, depression overcomes them and they feel that they don't have any assets! After going the rounds of job interviews, one college graduate with a degree in education, reported that she was almost ready to take a job in a pizza parlor. Job responsibilities at home can help these feelings of inadequacy and depression, while the nester plays the job-waiting game. However, the nester should also receive encouragement such as suggestions of job possibilities, if needed, in order to find meaningful work. Sometimes if too much leniency is given, the nester can become too selective in accepting a job and never really get serious about working.

When going to school. Some nesters seem to be making a career out of going to school. They keep changing their major and so need to spend extra time in college, or they get a degree in one field after another. Meanwhile, their parents are being asked to provide financial support. One mother writes, "John loves to study, and living at home has made it possible for him to advance academically. I sometimes accuse him of collecting college degrees!" Another nester is in the process of earning her third degree while she is working part-time.

There may be a fine line in the case of the permanent student, similar to the nester who isn't interested in work. Some nesters may be fearful of entering the job market and choose to find another area of study rather than join the work force. A frank discussion in either case should make this point clear. Is the nester avoiding reality by saying he or she wants to study yet another topic? Or does the nester really need help—financial and/or emotional—as he or she continues studying?

Many nesters find school a fun, comfortable place to be. One father claims his son "crammed" four years of college into seven years. This young man became very involved in his fraternity, holding the office of vice president. The position necessitated running meetings, assigning duties in the fraternity house and seeing that they were completed. Moreover, he joined the broomball team and discovered that this sport also took time away from studies. Somehow college continued year after year. During all this time, his dad sometimes became impatient. In retrospect, dad can take comfort that the skills his son acquired in these extracurricular activities became useful in his business career.

Some parents feel that their grown children are ungrateful. Often it helps keep things in perspective when we hear of a case in the extreme. Annie decided to sue her parents for more than $100,000 because they advised her to attend college. "The only way you'll have a real career," they told her, "is to get a college degree." Annie followed their advice, but she still hadn't found employment a year after graduation in her chosen field, music. She became upset because she spent $20,000 in tuition, room and board in addition to 10,000 hours studying. While attending school, she said, she lost over $16,000 in income. She tried to soften the lawsuit blow by stating, "I have nothing against my parents, really—I love them.

But I think they owe it to me because I wasted my time getting good grades when I could have been making money."

This is not an isolated case. In another family, there are two grown sons, ages 26 and 30. "They're older," says Mom, "and they are still home." The eldest son, an accountant, went back to earn his MBA degree. Now he is unhappy with accounting, blaming his folks for steering him into that field. One morning his mother saw him tuck an LSAT book (Legal Studies Aptitude Test) under his arm and head for the front door. "What's that book," she asked, "and where are you going?" He replied that he was going to look into law school, saying maybe he wanted to be an attorney. Outwardly mom didn't respond, but inwardly she wilted. Where had she and her husband gone wrong? With their son's mathematical skills, they thought he'd be a natural for accounting. They'd financed both his degrees and now he was still unfulfilled and blaming them besides!

In the first example, Annie's frustration in her inability to find work is evident, but now is not the time to cast bricks. Unemployment is devastating to one's self-esteem and one's pocketbook. When a family member is out of work, that's when the total support of the family is needed in the form of affirmation, encouragement and support.

Parents have the right and a responsibility to pass on information to their progeny based on their own experiences and knowledge. Young adults, however, also have the right to accept or reject advice. Once Annie had decided to accept their advice to attend college, it was then her decision, not theirs, to major in music.

The best way to ease tensions in similar instances is through communication. Parents should talk freely about feelings and resentments, and be open about expectations. Listen, trying to sense the motivation behind feelings. Then, weigh all of this information in the light of the current situation.

In the second example, a double degree, accounting and law, would make this young man very marketable. The parents and son could work out a compromise. They have several options. Since money seems to be a source of irritation, the son could attend law school nights and work part time, with the parents paying tuition and the son paying room and board. If he wants to study at a faster rate, he could attend full-time with the aid of a formal loan arrangement from his parents.

When the nester is handicapped. A 1992 Census Bureau report, "Statistical Brief on Disability," states that 3,282,000 adult children with disabilities live in their parents' homes. The Bureau's definition of handicapped includes physical, mental and emotional disabilities. This number is increasing because institutions for persons with disabilities are being phased out and many of these individuals are being returned to society or never committed in the first place.

Changes began occurring in the late 1960s and 1970s, when de-institutionalization was in full swing in the area of living arrangements for persons with handicaps. Since children and adults with disabilities are leaving public institutions or do not enter them at all, their presence is being felt and seen in our communities. The goal is to encourage those with disabilities to live lifestyles as close to their peers as possible. However, many disabled, some who are in their 40s, 50s and 60s, live in parental homes on a long-term basis. Others stay with relatives and some live independently with support.

People with disabilities are now claiming the right to develop relationships, to be a part of community life, and to take increased control over their own lives. Many need support services. These services are best when provided on an individual basis. "Whatever it takes" is commonly used as a guideline for helping the individual to be as independent as possible. Just because some people have disabilities doesn't mean that they can't be achieving what their peers are.

Support services help, depending on the families' needs. So families shouldn't close the door on services. Many families cope, or try to cope, without using services. In one home, the 48-year-old daughter had been cared for all her life, without support services, by her aging parents. She became injured and needed extra care, including lifting. However, when the father broke his hip, the mother alone could not take care of her daughter. In the ensuing crisis, the decision was made to place the daughter in a nursing home until she was healed.

However, if these parents had been aware of the help available, it was possible that the daughter could have remained at home with her mother, with personal care attendants coming in to help out as needed or, the daughter could have been moved to a group home or even her own apartment, with live-in personal care attendants.

Most parents who have children who are handicapped feel that they can never lay down their parenting; they will always have someone who is dependent upon them. The situation limits their retirement years and possibilities. Often, they have no vacations and travel is dependent upon the availability of respite care, which is temporary care of their offspring who is disabled.

"Our daughter, who is 20, has to be constantly supervised," writes one mother. "We always have to have a sitter when we go out. We have very little freedom. Sometimes we need a break. Our plans are to get her into a day program and eventually into a group home that has supervision, as she will never be independent enough to take care of herself."

One mother of a 20-year-old son who has Downs Syndrome writes, "Our son doesn't pose much difficulty. We arrange care for him to stay with other adult siblings if we need time away. It's very difficult to view him as an adult when his mental level is about 7 years. I fear the world out there when it comes to placing him in a different living situation. I would like to see my son in an apartment, duplex, or home with a few of his classmates, supervised by adults who have known him for some time, and in a neighborhood that is accepting of handicapped and safe to walk in, day or night."

Another mother of a 22-year-old daughter who has always lived in the parental home relates, "I would eventually like to see my daughter placed in a small group home, but for now we are 'playing it by ear'."

A first call for help should be to the local office of the Department of Human Services. The department will assign a social worker who will evaluate the family circumstances. There are in-home support services available to persons with disabilities under Title 19. Normally, governmental financial assistance is granted only if a family is below poverty level, but with disabilities these income levels are waived, making support services more accessible. Here are some considerations in living with a nester who has a handicap:

Assessment of needs and desires   *Self-care training*
Education   *Help with estate planning*
Career training   *Finding day programs*
Social interaction   *Personal futures planning**
Recreation and leisure   *Respite care*
Community participation   *Cooking and domestic training*
Personal care attendants

It is important to establish a circle of support that will last throughout an individual's lifetime, especially after parents are no longer able to provide care. The circle of support can include the person's family, relatives, friends, health care professionals, and government agencies. It can be a mistake for parents to assume that the siblings of the individual with handicaps will be able, or willing, to assume care after the parents are gone. So, coordinating the person's circle of support is, in most cases, the parent or guardian's job. An organization which can help coordinate all of this is Estate Planning for People with Disabilities (EPD).** This organization helps to develop a comprehensive life plan, which includes all of the above considerations.

---

*Estate Planning for People with Disabilities, 9001 E. Bloomington Freeway, Bloomington, MN 55420 (800) 487-5310

**Personal Futures Planning, "It's Never Too Early, It's Never Too Late", Metropolitan Council, Mears Park Center, 230 E. 5th St., St. Paul, MN 55101 (612) 291-6359

When postponing marriage. Marriage is one of the most common reasons offspring leave the family home. However, with weddings being put off until a later date, many young people are coming home or remaining home for longer periods, as the graph, *Marrying ages at first marriages in the United States, 1950-1991*, shows. [8]

In 1950, the median age for men marrying was 22.8 years, and for women it was 20.3. There was no change between 1950 and 1960. However, by 1979, both sexes were waiting about two years longer. Then in 1991, the median age of men marrying for the first time was 26.3 and for women it was 24.1. Remember, these are the median marrying age statistics. That means there were as many over these ages as under. So some even married later—much later than this chart shows.

Marrying ages at first marriages in the United States, 1950 - 1991

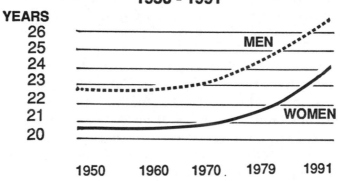

Why are young people marrying later? It could be because additional education and job training now are necessary to enable individuals to step into today's work force, where there is a greater demand for technical ability. In one family, the father grew up on a farm that did not have electricity until 1948. Yet, only 30 years later, technology had advanced so rapidly that he found it advantageous to obtain a home computer. Yes, young people do need more education now than they did 30 to 40 years ago to keep up with technology and have an employable skill. However, many young people feel that they can't afford both continued education and marriage, so they are postponing marriage. They feel that marriage is a luxury that they can't afford at present. They also fear the growing divorce rate, and want to be very, very certain that a person is the right one for them before entering into marriage.

Few women today expect not to work outside the home. They no longer stop working when they get married. Some also feel that they want to be skilled in a field before they enter marriage—just in case something goes wrong with the marriage relationship. One young woman said, "I'm going to make sure I'm always in a position to support myself and stand on my own before I enter into marriage, so that no matter what happens, I'll be all right." [9]

Parents needn't think that their nester is the only one who is not married! Some annoyed parents feel that their daughters are just being too selective. And in some cases this is true.

Many young people feel that they won't marry until "the right one" comes along. "He will have to be my equal," one young woman says. "That means he'll have to make at least as much money as I do and should be as well educated. He'll have to understand that my job is as important to me as his is to him." She hopes that her future husband likes to cook, is also neat, and that he likes her house. [10]

Because the social stigma against being single is no longer present, young people feel they can be more particular about a mate and are remaining single much longer. There's another reason many young women remain single: a shortage of men.

The 1990 Census Bureau says that between the ages of 25 and 49, women in the United States outnumber men by almost half a million. One of the contributing factors to this male shortage is the Vietnam War of the late 1960s and early 1970s. The total casualties were 155,419, mostly men, which includes 48,095 deaths. [11]

This shortage is even more severe for professional women looking for a husband. These women more than doubled in numbers from 1970 to 1990. They want to marry a man who is their equal or superior in finances, education and status in the community. They are finding that there just aren't enough men to go around who fulfill these criteria. As women are being educated to a greater degree, and as their earnings rise, this problem will intensify. "

Meanwhile, the women who are well educated are the least married."[12] They can't find a mate who lives up to their expectations.

Men's expectations of a mate are also high. "I've been told I expect too much," one young man said. "However, I feel if I can't have what I want, I may remain a bachelor forever. I'm looking for someone who is educated, intellectually mature, physically appealing, a professional person in my field or a related field, one who has a head on her shoulders, some good common sense and especially a feeling of responsibility—someone who is willing to share, to cooperate in a relationship."[13]

Some young men are looking for a companion. They place special emphasis on communication, compassion and loyalty. "I'm looking for someone who could be my best friend," one young man wrote. "Someone I could talk to and also be willing to listen to. Someone who is outgoing, loving and loyal. I want someone who is spontaneous and will allow me to be spontaneous. Someone who will allow me to express and experience all the different emotions, including feelings of weakness. And this is a problem. A lot of women that you run into don't like their men to show any weakness. It makes them feel insecure."[14]

So we can see that, for various reasons, young people are marrying later. This means that a certain portion of these unmarrieds are staying on in the parental home.

Reasons behind increased nester returns

Nesters are drawn to living at home because they enjoy home life and want to share their lives with their families. Another reason is financial. Many young people can't afford to live alone.

Other reasons are that young adults are saving money for their future, they want to form an adult relationship with their families, they have a need for the companionship of their family, or they want to mend a broken relationship.

Other nesters are home because they are out of a job, in school and can't afford rent, or don't feel the need to move because they aren't getting married.

CHAPTER FOUR

Benefits
and problems
of nesters

*"One night my husband and I sat down
and tried to figure out what the attractions
of living at home are—other than free laundry,
free rent, free toiletries, security, love,
a permanent address for mail, unlimited storage,
financing and loans, convention rooms for private parties
and entertaining, and guest privileges."*
— Humor columnist Erma Bombeck[1]

Families experience pluses and minuses when young adults nest. Parents delight in discovering that having their grown children at home can broaden their family interests, can mean shared family recreation, and can provide help with younger siblings. Conversely, nesting can also bring problems such as arguments or disputes over territory, time, possessions and sound. Small irritations grow, misunderstandings occur, and communication gaps widen. Some parents experience a stress on their marital bond.

Nesting advantages

Some families find that nesting broadens family interests. Life is often full, exciting, and challenging for a young nester. When they share some of this excitement around the dinner table or over coffee in the evening, it can expand the parents' world.

An example is a college nester who relates news from the academic world to parents. One student nester urged her mother to accompany her to a class at the local university. This mom was married at age 19, so she had not attended college, a fact which she often regretted. It was frightening for her to think of entering a university with over 50,000 students, countless buildings and many acres of land. Yet, because of her daughter's invitation she did, and had an opportunity to get a taste of college.

The large public-health class that mother and daughter attended together focused on the tragic sudden infant death syndrome (SIDS). Fifteen years earlier, this family had a son who died from SIDS, and the mother had since read everything she could find on the subject. As the professor discussed the subject, the mother eagerly followed the lecture, and often whispered answers to her daughter in response to the professor's questions. Finally, the professor asked a question that no student was able to answer. The daughter, suspecting that her mother knew the answer, urged her to raise her hand. Upon recognition by the professor, she responded with the correct reply. What an ego boost for this 40-year-old mother. The daughter, in turn, developed new respect for her mom.

Business-world nesters have jobs that, when shared with the family, can add luster to family life. One such nester was a booking agent for models. Through her job, the nester met famous, interesting people and she often told her parents about them. Then, too, when reading the newspaper, she told her family a little about the glamorous models pictured in the ads. She even got modeling jobs for some family members, including her grandparents.

Of course, grown sons or daughters who are not living at home can also provide stimulation because of their schooling or their jobs, but it happens more easily and naturally when they are nesting. So be open to suggestions from your grown children. Who knows what new direction your life make take?

One mother had her 26-year-old daughter, along with the daughter's 3-year-old son, and a 21-year-old son all move in to share their family life. "For three years I prayed to God to get my daughter out of an unhealthly live-in situation," Mom relates, "so how can I complain now that she's back home? Besides, she would have to be on welfare if she lived on her own and I feel that her son would suffer because of the stress they'd be living under. Our daughter needs the reinforcement of her family in order to properly care for her 3-year-old. She says she's learned a lot from me on the topic. But she needs to learn more as she doesn't always realize her son's needs and she needs to acquire more patience."

Mom continued that having a daughter and grandson living at home is difficult, but very rewarding. This mom feels that because her grown children are living at home, she is still able to offer needed direction and guidance. In fact, she feels that if her impoverished daughter and grandson didn't live at home she'd feel guilty. Why should she have a big, almost-empty house while they have sub-standard living? The minuscule rent the daughter pays helps out some, too. Moreover, the daughter needs to improve her housekeeping skills.

"I end up caring for her 3-year-old far too often," complains Mom, "and cleaning up his messes more than I should." Mom also laments that her daughter sleeps too late, but that she (the grandma) is up anyway so she ends up being in charge of the grandchild. This makes the daughter feel guilty, but she doesn't seem to be able to change her habit of oversleeping. As a trade-off, Mom suggested that she help out in the kitchen.

Nesting can mean shared family recreation. Some families complain that there is nothing that a family can do together once their children are grown.

However, many other families like their nesters to join in the family fun. One mother said that her grown daughter had to be coaxed to join in family recreation because she always felt she had to study and hadn't learned to relax. But others say that their adult offspring often join in the family relaxation.

Examples of shared family recreation

tennis	*television*	*traveling*
camping	*jigsaw puzzles*	*special events*
hunting	*ping pong & pool*	*visiting relatives*
fishing	*cards*	*dining out*

Only a few families say that their nester never or rarely joins in family recreation. One well-to-do family's recreational activities were reported in Fortune magazine. The Hubie Clark family included the father, mother, six children and three spouses of the children.

Mr. Clark planned and paid for an elaborate family vacation, a two-week cruise. He feels that if you plan an expensive enough trip, you can get almost every family to pull together and enjoy it. But he points out that the ability to enjoy it with the happiness and emotional experience that goes with such a trip is the difference. "And I do think that has happened in our family. Over the years we've been working to understand what's important to each member. I really think we could do the same thing around a camping trip in the mountains and have just as much fun."[2]

Unlike some executives, Clark has not sacrificed his family for his work. He has tried to use what he's learned about human relations in business to strengthen the family. While a lot of families do things together, Clark feels that few are able to talk things out without hostility or to resolve conflict before it hurts. "To be able to understand the needs of the human beings around you, and in some ways respond, is the heartbeat of a marriage and of a family relationship," Clark thinks. "Our kids are beginning to sense that."[3]

The Clark family is a unique instance; few families can afford a two-week cruise for 11 people. However, any family can make recreation plans to fit their own interests and budget. Family fun can be as elaborate as a cruise to work on improving family relationships, or it can be as simple as hot, buttered popcorn in the living room to celebrate a nester's new job.

A nester can help out with younger siblings. One mother reported that she carefully planned a 25th wedding anniversary weekend with her husband. The reservations were made months in advance at a romantic 19th century inn. For years, these parents hadn't felt comfortable leaving their large brood of nine. They always had a troublesome teenager who needed careful supervision. Finally, they felt they could get away for two days because their 25-year-old daughter was at home.

This jubilant couple left home Friday evening almost giddy with a new sense of freedom. However, at 10 the next day the phone call came. They were told not to worry, but the 17-year-old son was hospitalized and needed the parents' permission for the doctor to operate. What had happened? He fell, came the response. How? "I don't know," answered the daughter.

Later, much later, the full facts surfaced. Yes, the son had fallen, but that wasn't the whole story. Unbeknownst to their daughter, the son had gone to a kegger party held in an open field. When the under-age drinking group was surprised by the police, dozens of teenagers fled in all directions. The youth's foot landed in a gopher hole, he stumbled and fell, chipping his ankle. Because their older daughter was at home and in charge of the situation, this couple did not have to abandon their anniversary plans, although the accident did put a slight damper on their weekend.

But in perspective, we can see that there are many benefits to make nesting attractive: it's more fun than living alone, it's cheaper, and it allows many nesters to save money. It's a way for families to get to know each other as adults, it offers companionship, and it broadens family interests. Additionally, it's extra time to impart needed skills, it's an opportunity to mend damaged relationships, it's a haven to those offspring, and it's also great to share family fun. No wonder 18 million American adult sons and daughters are nesting.

Nesting problems

Young people are drawn to, return to, or remain in, the parental home for various advantages. However, the consequences of nesting can often be a host of problems—both large and small. Life with an adult offspring can raise specific problems that are unique to nesting.

Some young people forget the need to be considerate to other family members. Then, irritations blossom and misunderstandings can arise. In addition, nesting can cause stress on the parental marriage bond. It's sometimes difficult to have various age groups living in one house. At times, the atmosphere can get overheated and relationships can get strained and tense. We all want to live orderly, predictable, calm lives, but life with a nester oftentimes is the very opposite. It's an added burden to have an adult child living at home, especially if that person's life is in turmoil—which is frequently the case with a nester.

If we analyze the problems and then think and talk about them, we will find that generally there is a workable solution. By looking at other families and how they cope with conflicts, we can learn how to overcome these problems.

Vicky, a mother of 15 children, seven born to her and her husband and eight adopted, comments, "Sometimes I feel that other people think it doesn't take much intelligence to run a family. On the contrary, it takes a brilliant person to do this, because of the multiplicity of problems that arise. I had a profession previous to marriage, so I know a profession has its own headaches, its own discipline. But that profession wasn't nearly as taxing as being a homemaker. I know that the grass isn't greener on the other side of the fence. I've been there. Sure, it's work being a parent, but anything worthwhile requires time and effort."[4]

The **need to be considerate**. In an extended family household, a lack of privacy and freedom can be just as confining for the nesters as for the other family members. A nester's peers who live independently can revel in self-involvement that a nester doesn't share. Instead, the nester has to learn to be considerate, to cooperate, and to respect others' rights in various areas.

Nesting problems to be aware of:

Space and territory:
Leaving clothes, dirty dishes, or books scattered throughout the home.
Being aware that certain areas of the home may be private domain (bedrooms, closets, etc.).

Time:
Being a "last minute" person
Insisting that everyone help find a lost item
Sharing bathroom time
Asking someone to mend a piece of clothing at the last minute or prepare a quick meal when one is late for work.
Insisting, "I need help right now!"
Being on the telephone too long

Possessions:
Borrowing clothes
Borrowing a car
Borrowing food for a party

Sound:
Disrupting volume of radio or stereo
Receiving telephone calls late at night

As an example of consideration, we can look at a family in which a daughter in her mid-20s returned home. She had no car, so, to get to work, she was allowed to use her mother's car. One day, the carless mother desperately needed groceries, and had to use a bicycle to get to the store. Pushing a bicycle heavily laden with groceries up a steep hill was not her favorite pastime—not at all what she had envisioned herself doing when she reached her 50th year.

Still, this mother, out of consideration for her daughter, was willing to make the sacrifice of her car. Sometimes we have to put aside our own personal wants, feelings, and needs because there are other people in the house to be considered.

One grown daughter who had never had a weight problem gained 40 pounds in the six months before her marriage. She and her fiance were living with her recently-divorced dad to save money, but also to give comfort and support to her dad in his difficult adjustment period.

Her weight piled on because her dad and her fiance worked different hours and couldn't eat their main meal at the same time. The daughter cooked for both. The problem arose because both dad and fiance wanted her to eat with them. She acquiesced to be sociable. The wedding dress purchased months before began to look smaller and smaller.

Possibly the daughter could have eaten every other day with her fiance and on alternate days with her dad. In this particular case, however, the issue over meals couldn't be resolved, the young couple moved into their own apartment prematurely, months before the marriage ceremony. The wedding dress had to undergo extensive alterations.

One mother decided to clean out her daughter's basement bedroom after she left for her second year at college. The mother had promised one of her younger daughters, who shared a room with another sister, that she could use the recently emptied bedroom. When Mom tried to open the bedroom door, it wouldn't budge. Shocked, she realized that someone had drilled a lock onto the door and it was now secured.

Angrily, she phoned her older daughter at school and demanded an explanation. The daughter promptly replied that she had asked her boyfriend to put the lock on. In answer to her mother's "Why?" she responded, "Well you always told me to clean my room. So, I figured it was my room. I'll be back for Thanksgiving weekend, and Christmas and Easter breaks!"

Mom had the lock removed, she packed the clothes and paraphernalia into carefully labeled boxes, and the younger sister moved in. How had this happened, a stunned mother asked herself? Sure, I said "clean your room," but I didn't really mean it was her room! Maybe all those years I should have said, "clean the bedroom you sleep in," or "clean the red carpet bedroom."

The following is a story the author heard while she was a featured guest on a four-hour, call-in radio program. Two adult sons, both in their late 20s and living at home with their parents, were having a problem. The older son had just been discharged from the Navy, hadn't found a job yet, and only recently moved back. The two-bedroom parental home was small and quarters were cramped. Since both the bedrooms were full, the former Navy man slept on the living room sofa. But the younger son liked to watch television until late at night, and the older son, accustomed to morning reveille, retired early so that he could get an early start on the job search. He couldn't sleep with the TV blaring.

Hearing the radio talk show centering on adults living in the parental home, the elder son called in to complain about his younger brother—how he blasted the TV late at night. The author listened sympathetically, suggesting how they might come to an agreement about TV hours and volume. Later, during the same radio show, there came another call, this one from the younger brother. He'd heard his older brother complaining on the air about his TV watching and wanted to get his side heard. His brother, he complained, "slobbed" up the living room, leaving the remains of his snacks littered about the room, dropping his dirty socks next to the chair, and scattered the newspapers all about.

The author again listened empathetically, then suggested how the brothers might negotiate an agreement about both the TV and the living room's cleanliness. The brothers each called two more times during the lengthy program before they finally came to a final compromise, each promising that they'd try harder to be more considerate of each other. After all, living back at home was only temporary, and they'd try to make the best of a difficult, but short, situation.

Small irritations can grow. It isn't usually the big things that cause irritations in living with a nester—it's often the little things. In this respect, nesting is very similar to the marriage relationship.

One mother was quite irritated that her 21-year-old daughter frequently forgot to turn off her curling iron. She also sometimes went to work leaving behind a red-hot iron after she pressed her clothes. This daughter always left home looking neat, clean and beautiful, which required a great deal of time. But turning off small appliances didn't seem to be on her mind as she prepared to leave the house. This happened again and again, despite all her mother's efforts to remind her daughter. It got to be such a common occurrence that the mother automatically checked these two items each morning after her daughter left for work. This irritated the mother and she found herself becoming increasingly resentful.

So, one morning this mother phoned the utility company to find out just how much it would cost if either of these two items were left on for 24 hours—the length of time they would be left on until her daughter used them again. Much to her amazement, mother discovered that it cost only nine cents to run the curling iron for 24 hours. However, the pressing iron was a different story—$1.48 for the same time. On the basis of that information, Mother decided it was inconsequential to worry about the curling iron, as long as it wasn't left on a towel or any place where it could be a fire hazard. Instead, she concentrated on the pressing iron, and relayed this financial information to her daughter. Thereafter, she found a decided improvement in the frequency of left-on appliances.

This mother has learned to home in on important areas and ignore trivial matters. She related that she found herself thinking, "Why was I worrying about an insignificant nine cents? As long as she leaves it in a safe place, that curling iron isn't worth making a fuss about!" Lesson learned: the reaction to a problem should be in proportion to the severity of the problem itself. Pick your wars carefully!

One mother of a student-son was happy to help him out by allowing him to live at home rent-free. She and her husband knew he didn't have the funds to pay both tuition and rent. There was one bone of contention, though, between mother and son. She didn't mind doing his laundry; she asked only that he gather it up daily and toss it in the clothes hamper. Apparently this wasn't on his priority list, for he didn't get around to it.

Mom decided to stop gathering and laundering his clothes. This was a radical move on her part as she felt that cleanliness was next to Godliness. She shut his bedroom door so she wouldn't have to look at the dirty laundry strewn about. Finally, her son ran out of clean underwear. Shocked, he complained to Mom. "I'll wash anything," she replied, "that's in the hamper." For a while he recycled his dirty underwear, but finally decided to use the hamper.

Another mother related that whenever she and her husband go away on vacation they always arrange for at least several of their grown sons to stay at their home. "They are mostly trustworthy," Mom writes, "except for the time they left the iron on. Fortunately, the ensuing small fire was easily contained and damage was minimal."

Not only do parents, brothers and sisters of nesters experience irritations, but so do the nesters themselves while they are living at home.

One 22-year-old full-time college student, who is working part-time in the accounting department of a large hotel, related that he is happy to be living at home and that there is very little friction in the family. However, he continued, his mother complains about his spelling, and this bothers him. In reading through his questionnaire answers, it soon became evident why his mother was objecting. He had an innovative approach to spelling: "iceolated" and "obinion." His mother was probably trying to make him aware of this problem, but did nagging help her son? Possibly, mother should slack off pressure, as her son is well aware of this academic deficiency by now.

It's so easy for parents to fall into a habit of nagging their nesters. Young people complain that parents nag about late hours, messy rooms, style of dress, table manners and the way they drive the car. Most parents believe it's for their nesters' own good. But how much will, or can, these nesters change now that they are adults?

Humor columnist Erma Bombeck writes about the little annoyances caused by nesters. She says that when all her children grew up and moved out, she treated herself to a light green carpet in the spare bedroom. She writes, "Three months later, one of my children moved back with, among other things, a set of drums that leaked oil. My celery green carpet looked like a left-over. When he left we had it cleaned and began again. The next prodigal son brought a dog that had a sofa wish, a car that was not garage trained and leaked oil when it was parked there and used towels like they were disposable nose tissues that popped up automatically in a box. The next one to return let me use my own phone, but kept hours like a fireman."[5] As Bombeck illustrates, looking for and seeing the humor in a situation helps us to live with annoyances.

In addition to annoying habits of nesters, parents may have to learn how to cope with unexpected crises. A mother of two nesting sons felt that once she had adjusted to seeing her sons fixing carburetors on the kitchen table, she'd be able to face up to anything else they'd do. However, her resolve was definitely tested when the following incident occurred. One Saturday she had cleaned the house spotlessly in preparation for Sunday dinner guests. The next morning, she went to church and returned home to find that two freshly painted shock absorbers were baking in the oven which she needed to cook dinner.[6]

It is sometimes difficult living with blood relatives, but living with in-laws can be even harder. Careful consideration should be given ahead of time before living together is attempted. Married nesters can create unique problems. One mother suggested her daughter and son-in-law move in with her because they were having trouble saving money for a down payment on a home of their own. But very quickly problems arose. Mother and son-in-law were not getting along at all! Finally, after six months, the mother told her daughter, "Either he goes, or you both go." Her daughter stayed, but the husband left.[7]

A stepfather wrote that he and his stepchildren have a bone of contention between them. It seems minor, but nonetheless, it is extremely irritating to him. He has asked his wife's children to use a sheet on the sofa when they sleep there. "We feel strongly about this," Dad relates, "but they don't see it as important." As in the marital bond, it's not always the big things that cause a rift. It's the little everyday annoyances that chip away at a relationship.

Many business people have found that it is a lot easier to get results if you make it as painless as possible to promote cooperation. Why can't we transfer this idea over into our home life? Could this problem be solved if a sheet was kept under the sofa, or the sofa pillows? The sheet would always be handy and it is possible it would be used as desired by the parents.

Misunderstandings. Underlying misunderstandings can cause havoc in family relationships. Jack blew up in anger one Saturday at his 21-year-old daughter, Corky, for not helping with cleaning. She lashed back, "Well, I pay rent, but no one bothered to tell me last week that the rust remover on the water system wasn't working. I washed my clothes and three blouses were ruined." Believing this was off the subject, Jack didn't want to listen and walked away from her. At lunchtime, she was still too upset to eat. After thinking that

Corky would probably be angry at him for a week, and seeing that his wife was distraught over the two of them fighting, Jack decided to talk to Corky. They talked it out, working out both the problem of the chores and the water softener, and then the whole family had lunch together peacefully.

Corky and her father really have a deeper misunderstanding, though, about room and board. Corky thinks that the $25 a week she pays is enough, but her father disagrees. Given this disagreement, there will probably be another fight tomorrow or next week. It would be so much better if Jack and Corky could talk over their differences about room and board than to ignore this underlying problem. Corky's position is that $25 is a lot to pay for room and board since she is usually on a diet and doesn't eat that much anyway. She also believes her parents would have to heat her bedroom whether she or her sister slept in it. And besides, her parents know that she makes only $1,000 a month before deductions!

On the other hand, Jack realizes it would probably cost his daughter $225 a month for apartment rental if she shared it with a friend, groceries would be at least an additional $95, and other items like utilities, toiletries and laundry would easily cost Corky double or triple what she now pays for room and board. Also, if Corky did have an apartment, she would still have to do the same cleaning chores she was balking at in her parents' home. What Jack and Corky really need is to discuss their various viewpoints, let each other see where they are coming from, and set a compromise price for room and board.

One war-bride mom, divorced from her husband, went to her treasured cache of 25 bottles of very expensive German wine she had brought to America. She was having some friends in for a dinner party and wanted to chill some wine. To her dismay and anger she found her cupboards were bare.

She confronted her 22-year-old son, who had been living with her. He readily admitted to drinking her wine, even sharing some of it with his friends. She told him that if he wanted something to drink that desperately she would have loaned him some money to go buy some beer or whatever they needed! But why had they taken her expensive, aged wine? He said that he didn't use it all at once, just a bottle here and there. He hadn't realized he'd taken it all. He was sorry.

That was the last straw in this fragile mother/son relationship. She told him he had to leave. He realized that he had stolen her valued property and now left knowing he had to suffer the consequences. After a few months, he called and asked if he could stop over. She invited him to supper, but not to stay. During the meal he told Mom just how desperate he was. He just couldn't get his life straightened out. "Can't I stay again," he pleaded, "just for a short while?"

Mom thought it over and said she'd give him an answer after they'd eaten their chocolate cake. By then Mom had formulated her offer. She'd allow him to sleep in the unfinished basement if he wanted to fix up a bedroom area there for himself. She would lock the basement door, barring him from using the upstairs, where she kept all her important goods. He could use an old mattress which was stored in the basement, and she'd let him use some of her old blankets. But that's as far as she'd go.

No, he couldn't use her kitchen. He couldn't even use her bathroom, she added, handing him an empty, five-quart, covered ice cream container saying he could use this bucket and empty it at the corner gas station. "You violated my home," she said, "you'll have to earn my trust before you can live with me again. Once in a while I'll invite you to eat with me, but that's it!"

Grandparenting. Several parents, who have both their adult child and grandchild living in the parental home, experience problems with authority and discipline. One grandma states, "My daughter doesn't pick up the baby enough, and doesn't pay him the right kind of attention." She says she finds herself being the real mother many times and resents the imposition of the role because she feels too old to be doing this again.

Another grandmother tries to make her daughter recognize her motherly responsibilities, but it's often a struggle for the grandmother. Once, in the middle of the night when the baby cried, the grandfather had to hold down his wife and let the young mother get up to care for the crying child. She found it hard to go against her instinct and not run to help.

In still another three-generation home, a grandmother complains because her husband hides behind books to avoid problems.

Sometimes these multi-generational family units have to resort to the courts to collect child support in an effort to force the fathers of the grandchildren to help with the financial struggles.

Some grandparents in Philadelphia and elsewhere have formed support groups for emotional and spiritual help through their churches to deal with the problem of in-home grown children and grandchildren. This support group also gives information about social agencies that offer further assistance. The care-giving group stresses that the grandchildren are the responsibility of the parents, not the grandparents. "I can't control what the parents do," says one grandmother, "except when the baby is disturbing our rest. Then I raise hell!"[8]

Communication gaps. In a later chapter, the problem of communicating will be dealt with in depth, but here it will be briefly noted that problems in communicating can be some of the consequences of nesting. The signals that families traded throughout the growing-up years are no longer applicable after the offspring are grown.

Parents can't issue orders to their young adults in the same way they did to their children when they were young and expect them to be obeyed automatically. Nesters are now adults and should be making more of their own decisions. This does not mean that house rules need not apply to the nester. It does mean that families have to discover new ways of relating to one another, of realizing what is expected of both parents and nesters. When expectations are unclear, misunderstandings and hurt feelings are inevitable.

"I am forever biting my tongue," one mother with a nesting son writes. Maybe what she didn't quite realize was that, as one adult to another, there needs to be a clarification of expectations, perhaps a modification of rules, to fit the needs of both parents and nesters. There obviously will be a period of adjustment after the nester reaches adulthood, but as one mother said, "If all parties involved feel very positively about the idea of living together, I do think it can work."

Stress on the parental marriage bond. A problem that is often unspoken with grown children living in the family home is a lessening of the intimacy between parents, as they struggle to fit another adult into their daily lives.

Dealing with problems relating to their nester can sometimes cause serious difficulties between parents. One author writes that a family household with grown children creates a radically different set of emotional arrangements, with a strong likelihood of a considerably diluted relationship between spouses.[9]

For example, one spouse may feel differently about a topic, such as room and board, than the other. Also, there may be intense friction between a parent and a nester which is so draining that there isn't much emotional feeling left over for the spouse.

These problems should be talked out, with everyone realizing that they are transitory. Eventually, the nester will move out and the tensions between parents will ease. Once again they'll be alone together with lots of time for just themselves.

One father with three nesters states, "Having adult offspring at home is an almost constant source of stress to us, as parents, which adversely affects our marriage. Financially, they don't bear anywhere near their share of expenses (groceries, car expenses, phone bills, laundry costs, etc.). There is always a conflict over use of resources such as cars, telephone, TV, stereo and bathroom. It is very difficult to daily witness their irresponsible behavior and to suffer along with them as consequences of their behavior and value systems surface. Furthermore, our younger children get upset when they see their older siblings coming home after obviously having had too much to drink."

Dad summarized his feelings by saying, "I'm not happy to have these grown youngsters at home, but I'm accepting it. I have mixed feelings. I'd like to be rid of them, but fear for their spiritual/moral well-being without parental control, even though it seems they should be old enough to be on their own."

One set of parents, whose 19-year-old son is living at home, relates that they are under pressure from two disgruntled sons-in-law. These in-laws have voiced their opinion that they feel the live-in son is being pampered and spoiled. The criticism became so constant that the father, with difficulty, finally had to inform his sons-in-law that this matter was just none of their business.

One mid-20s nester was surprised to discover that his parents still had an active love life, despite the fact that they were in their late 50s. When Mom and Dad stated that they wanted and really needed some time alone together, he needed to have this explicitly explained. After the initial shock, he adjusted to this new information with a warm glow. He felt good to realize that his parents still shared that part of their lives. So many of his friends' parents were divorced that he appreciated his mom's and dad's togetherness.

In another family, the marriage had deteriorated, and the wife was decidedly bored. So she turned to her only child, a nester son, for companionship. He and his friends, one of whom had also moved in with them, provided most of her conversation. Meanwhile, she had little communication with her husband. When they did talk, they avoided personal issues and topics that touched on feelings and opinions. He left early in the morning to go to work, and when he came home around 6 p.m., the family immediately ate supper. After that, the husband watched television and then went to bed. Without the conversation and companionship of her son and his friends, she felt she wouldn't have gotten her emotional needs fulfilled. But what will happen when the nester eventually leaves home?

On the other hand, when there are problems between the spouses, the nester may try to solve them. One nester wrote that he had a tendency to play "marriage counselor" for his parents. He thought he was offering infinite wisdom about how his parents should treat one another. That didn't work, he reported, because whenever he tried, it usually ended with both parents being hostile toward him.

Pluses and minuses of nesting

We can see that parents, as well as nesters, can gain a great deal from living with adult offspring.

It's beneficial to concentrate on the happy aspects and advantages of nesting, for then life appears rosier. If there is a tendency for a problem to arise, and everyone is aware of this tendency, the family is less likely to let that problem keep recurring if they have a positive outlook. Problems resulting in life with a nester need to be faced and resolved at an early stage, or else these problems can multiply.

There are certain irritating habits of nesters and certain inflexibilities of parents, that may need to change. But if a family is aware of problems, they can discuss them and try to solve them. At least there's no hope of solving a problem unless everyone is first aware that a problem exists.

CHAPTER FIVE

Independence and maturity

"In the parent's mind, a child grows, but does not age."
—Columnist Sydney Harris[1]

Everyone, it seems, is worried about the long-term effects of nesting. Some psychologists and sociologists are concerned that nesters will stagnate by living at home. Some parents worry that they may be clinging to their adult children and hindering their growth. Other parents worry that they are pushing their young adults out of the nest too soon.

No matter what we're worried about, these are important questions we need to ask ourselves. Will our nesters become independent and mature adults while living at home, or is it necessary for them to move out in order to grow? Many of us ask ourselves if nesting will have a positive or negative long-range effect on our grown children—and we're not sure of the answer. That's because what we find is different for all of us.

Independence and maturity vs. dependency and immaturity?

Nesters want to be independent, and parents want their adult children to become independent. But what does this mean? *Webster's Dictionary* offers one view:

*In-de-pen-dence: not subject to the control of another, able to act
on one's own authority, not having to rely on another person or thing,
a person unwilling to be subject to or under obligation to another,
resenting control, shunning advice, uninfluenced by any other person or thing, standing
by oneself, not dependent on another for support,
either possessing or earning means of support.*[2]

In addition, *Roget's Thesaurus* offers a few insights into what independence means: self-governing, freedom, self-reliant, unconnected, separate, or self-sufficient.[3] With these definitions, we can see a little more clearly what comprises independence and how it can be fostered.

Then there's the subject of maturity. The dictionary defines maturity as "brought by natural process to completeness of growth and development; full-grown; ripe or pertaining to a condition of full development." The thesaurus uses the synonym "adult." Psychoanalyst Anna Freud defines being mature as "to have the capacity to work and to love."[4] It is clear that our nesters need to be independent, and that they also need to become mature, emotionally stable and sensitive.

How can we tell whether our nester is moving in the right direction, or whether he or she is remaining dependent and immature? The dictionary defines dependence as: "a state of being supported by others, living at the expense of others, governed by, rely on, contingent on, conditioned by or connected with others." Immature means: "not arrived at full development, unripe, unfinished, youthful, not yet mature."

Types of nesters

With the above definitions it will be easier to assess whether a nester is independent, responsible and mature. In order for adult offspring to become truly independent, they must find their own identity—a realistic image of themselves. In finding their own identity, Canadian Professor Marci James states that our offspring fall into four different categories:[5]

1. **Foreclosures:** these offspring commit themselves to their parents' views without ever questioning. This type tends

to live at home for longer periods than the other types.

2. Diffusers: these offspring seem aimless, having no set vocation or ideological direction. They never really had a home in the first place, and they talk of feeling abandoned.

3. Moratoriers: these offspring remain uncertain about their own identity. They are always in the process of leaving, symbolically packing their bags, full of questioning doubts about their own identity.

4. Achievers: these offspring question the views of their parents, go through a crisis and find a self-chosen career goal and ideology. They have grown up by having gone through a period of questioning. Their values may perhaps be the same as their parents but at least they've gone through a stretch of experimenting with alternatives.[6]

If we can pinpoint what category our own nesters fall into, we may be able to understand, guide, and help our nesters on their road to independence.

Types of parents

In understanding nesters, it is important to examine types of parents that form the nesters. In identifying with one or more of these parental types, it will be possible to have a better perspective when relating with nesters.

The authoritarian parents. Authoritarian parents have a tendency to see their children, regardless of age, as their property, the way they regard an automobile or a television set. They order their children's behavior as they would any other object over which they wish to have control. If a parent is the authoritarian type, there's bound to be trouble when the child reaches the teens, and on into adulthood! An authoritarian parent issues directives and expects them to be obeyed. When the child was young, this parent was able to dictate an order and the child was compelled to obey. Some parents maintain, even after the child is an adult, that: "As long as he is under my roof, what I say goes!" However, when that child reaches adulthood, the nester usually feels he or she does not have to obey a parental order. He or she no longer will continue to play the role of a subservient robot.

Some authoritarian parents are too dominant and their adult offspring go through life beaten into submission. A nester who blindly carries out an order is not learning to be independent. Is this really what the parent wants?

Extreme authoritarian parents will drive a wedge between themselves and their children. Let's look at Mr. Smith, who routinely issues orders to his five children and expects instant, exact obedience. For example, when the boys were told to wash the family car, they were allotted only two buckets of water, told to use both sides of the sponge and wipe in a horizontal direction. As the boys grew up, they began to rebel, and as soon as they were able, they left the family home and severed all ties with their father. These children still come home to visit—but only with their mother and only when they know that their father will not be home.

Another example of a parent who is too authoritarian is one who still insists on ordering each detail of his grown off-spring's life. For instance, he insists that he alone knows what type of car or suit his son should buy—and where he should buy it.

The permissive parent. On the other hand, being permissive can spell trouble too, because this type of parent views owner-ship as a family affair. The children of permissive parents are allowed full use of all family belongings.

However, when these children become adults, this system is no longer effective because they "require" the family car, a brother's new shirt, or a mother's free time. ("But you aren't doing anything important, Mom, so can't you fix my jeans? I have to leave in seven minutes, and I really want to wear them!") These nesters will often expect tuition paid to the col-lege of their choice or free room and board even though they may have a good-paying job.

All too often the nester of a permissive parent will use the family car without permission and without refilling the gas tank, because he or she feels that it belongs to the family and he or she is part of the family. Many nesters of permissive parents have a difficult time learning responsible use of their parents' goods and time.

Parents who are either strongly permissive or authoritarian may need to find new ways of communicating, once their children become adults. Authoritarian parents may need a new awareness that their children are now adults and must begin to make their own decisions. Permissive parents may need a new awareness that their children are now adults and must begin to supply their own needs.

Neither the authoritarian nor the permissive parent is helping the child grow to be an independent person. But worse than the authoritarian parents or permissive parents is a mix, one of each!

The permissive parent feels that the other parent is too hard or tough on the "children" even though they really are adult ("You'll drive the children away from us and the house.") The authoritarian parent feels that the other parent is coddling the children ("They'll never grow up if you keep giving them everything that they ever need or even want.")

There is disagreement between the parents regarding how to relate to the children. This difference of opinion ripples throughout the family and is felt by everyone. This combination of permissive and authoritarian parents causes problems when children are minors, but once they become adults these problems are exacerbated.

Some families may not identify with the above types of parents. If so, they may be able to relate to the middle-of-the-road parent. This type of parent will allow his or her offspring to choose a household job from among many, with a time deadline for completion of the task. Another example of a middle-of-the-road parent is one who has a curfew with a known punishment for any violation. Nesters from middle-of-the-road parents will certainly find it easier to become independent.

Steps toward independence

Slowly, the offspring begins to take control of his or her life, first making small decisions, then larger ones. It's a gradual process.

Many offspring take quite a long time to become independent. They do it in steps—termed the Revolving Door Syndrome. They find numerous reasons to leave the parental home—a visit to a cousin's home, a vacation, time living on campus, traveling, or apartment living for various time spans. Generally, each time they leave it's for a longer period. But many do keep returning. When the break is finally made, the step is hardly noticed, since it was so gradual. For some nesters, this gradual leave-taking works well. For others, a sharp, quick break suits them fine.

Psychologist Arthur Maslow agrees and suggests that leave-taking doesn't have to be done in one big leap—it can be gradual. He feels that telephoning, visiting back and forth, dropping in to use the washing machine, and even accepting furniture from the folks' basement, makes the separation easier.[7]

One family kept what was jokingly referred to as a "free store" in a basement storage area. Unused, outdated furniture was kept there and could be had for the asking. Sometimes, Mom reported, even friends of their children came to the free store.

Psychologist Howard Halpern explains it this way: "Development is not a straight line... A step backward may follow two steps forward. You may have to take the wrong step in order to know the right step. You may discover after you move out that leaving was premature and that you need to return home for a while. Or, some offspring may stay at home, but realize that they can't be happy or adult as long as they do remain at home. All our trials and errors help us to work out the balance of closeness and distance that will work for us."[8]

One mother writes about her son: "He moved out when he was 19, moved back when he was 21 and out again at 23. He wanted badly to live independently, which eventually he did, but it is still a struggle. I wish he would move back at home where life would be easier for him, but he is fiercely independent."

Parents suffer right along with offspring in their fight toward independence.

Another writer, Grace Weinstein, describes it as a seesaw—going up and down, back and forth between the security that one receives from her parents and the independence that she can have on her own. The parents teeter-totter too between holding on to their offspring and letting go.[9] Some days the seesaw dips one way, other days it drifts in the opposite direction.

Growing up and forming our own identity is a process or a series of steps that one takes. It's never quite done or complete. We hope to continue to grow, learn and change throughout our lives. Sometimes it's a struggle—somewhat like a chick breaking its way out of its eggshell: a small peck here and a bigger peck there. It's painful oftentimes, but satisfying and challenging too, when we can see growth and progress in ourselves.

For many offspring, it's a real struggle to break away, physically and emotionally, because they feel tied to their parents who loved, protected and guided them from infancy onward. It's hard to cut the cord.

Parents and offspring should be alert to the fact that the time of leave-taking is often fraught with conflict. One mother reported that the summer before her daughter left for her freshman year at college was the first time they had ever had any real disagreements. A study of 142 Yale freshmen showed that anxiety and anger often accompanied an artificial deadline for leaving home.

The study stated that anger served as a separating function. It's easier for a nester to leave home if he or she is angry. "The stronger the fear of not being able to sever the umbilical cord," the researcher reported, "the greater the intensity of anger before leaving." Female emotions in this area were more intense than those of males. Anxiety and aggression toward the parents seemed to be a normal part of the transition of leaving home and becoming independent.[10]

The offspring is pulling away, yearning to find an autonomous identity, but feeling, very powerfully, the dependence he or she has had on his parents. The parents want to protect and hold onto their offspring, yet they know that they must let go. It's a push and pull situation, according to psychiatrist Daniel Goleman.[11]

Difficult steps

It's harder for some offspring to travel the road toward independence than for others. In some cases, an artificial deadline may help—such as college entrance or turning 18 or 21—as long as it's not strictly enforced. After all, independence and maturity don't jump into their suitcase as the youngster closes the front door! Be prepared when the deadline arrives, however: some offspring may not be ready to leave. And if they're pushed out, anyway, it can be devastating for them.

Suzie, a woman in her early 20s who appeared on the Phil Donahue Show, said: "My father is a strong believer in the idea that when one of his kids turns 18, that child moves out. So, I moved out at 18, but I couldn't support myself. So, I got married and had a baby. Then I got divorced. After that it was even worse—I was a single parent! So, I got married again and had another baby. Now I have two children, who I hope will grow up perfectly independent, but I would never, never tell them they're not welcome at home. If any time they wanted to come home, they're always welcome."

Phil questioned her, "You got married because you were thrown out?"

Suzie responded, "Oh, I don't want to blame my father, okay?"
But Phil continued, "But it certainly did encourage you to hook up?"

Affirmative reply. Phil then commented that he felt "there are far too many marriages that are formed in order to get out of the house—far too many marriages formed out of lack of parental support."[12]

So it may be wise to think twice before setting an inflexible deadline for departure.

"With no clear social norm, how can parents know whether they are pushing their children out the door too soon or erring in the opposite direction, clinging too long to their children?" Daniel Goleman asks in *Psychology Today*. Frederick Coons, a former director of the psychological counseling service at the University of Indiana, says it's harder for girls, only children, and youngest children to leave home.

However, variations from individual to individual may be enormous and, for many young people, the passage actually is far smoother than psychologists ever envisioned. Success or failure in the venture may depend as much on the parents' feelings about their own lives as on the resources of the young people themselves.[13] Are the parents able to allow the offspring to leave without objections? Do the parents have full lives on their own without needing the presence of their children? Are the offspring prepared to face the world apart from the parents?

One mother of nine children writes, "I firmly believe a child at 18 is not an adult and ready to live in the outside world today. He may think he is, but in reality, he isn't. A gradual weaning away from home, parents and family is necessary. When they do strike out on their own and 'fail' to make it because it's premature, they come back home for that needed security, confidence building, growing up, maturing time. Most importantly, they need to know they are still loved and accepted.

"Making a mistake can be a growing experience, if one learns from it. Failing at something saps their confidence, and inadvertently, they come back home to regroup. Most often they don't realize why they are coming home. On the surface it's finances, but it usually is much deeper than that. I realize some teens are more ready at 18 than others, but most aren't mature at that age."

It is interesting to note, though, that a 1976 study by the American Council of Life Insurance showed that young adults with only a high school diploma (as compared to a college degree), young married couples, and those from a lower-income background are more likely to be self-sufficient and to seek a second job in times of need. College graduates, singles, and those from more affluent backgrounds are more inclined to turn to, and rely upon, their parents for help.[14] This may be because lower income families are not able to give financial help and so the grown children don't expect it.

The philosophy of weaning a baby from the breast can very easily be applied to adult nesters. La Leche League, an organization devoted to teaching good mothering through breast feeding, holds this philosophy toward weaning: "Don't offer, but don't refuse." That is, if the mother feels it is time that the baby weans, she shouldn't offer the breast, but if the baby indicates he or she wants to nurse, she shouldn't refuse. It's a painless, natural and pleasant method of weaning. Weaning does eventually occur, when the baby is ready.

Like these weaning mothers, we don't want to keep our offspring dependent on us beyond what is good for them. But we also don't want to refuse to help them. So if a family is able to accommodate an adult offspring, La Leche League's slogan of "don't offer, but don't refuse" may be a good guide.

"Parents sometimes have a peculiar way of telescoping time," write Comer and Quinby in *Mademoiselle* magazine. "Despite the fact that you are obviously old enough to be making your own decisions, your parents may still occasionally become tangled in their memories of you as a child and want to keep helping you." It's really difficult for many parents to make the transition of seeing their offspring change from a child to an adult.[15]

A possible reason for this difficulty may be that families are set up for dependency. After all, the primary function of the family is to care for children. It's difficult for parents to change their frame of reference and to view their children as adults, just because they have turned [18].

Even when the transition is made, the situation can still be very trying. Parents see a living, breathing adult in front of them, but many wonder why this offspring isn't in the outside world taking care of himself or herself, like other adults they know.

It's just as hard for some offspring because they have been dependent upon their parents for 18 years. It can be difficult for some of them to make the transition from dependence to independence.

To get a better idea of independence/dependence, take this little quiz on the following page. Check the degrees of maturity possessed by the individuals described below. Read the quiz and then choose a number from one to 10 which denotes the degree of maturity you feel the young person possesses. Number 1 denotes extreme dependency, number 2 less dependency, and on up to number 10, which denotes complete independency.

Independence / dependence quiz

A. Nester helps out with expenses only when he's working, frequently sleeps late after he's been out having a few beers with his friends. Doesn't get along with other family members, nor help with any chores around the house.

B. Offspring lives away from home, has a good job, car, and apartment, but keeps such a messy place that he has to wade through the mess. Offspring always washes his clothes at his parents' place.

C. Nester contributes part of her income to household, helps with daily chores such as cleaning, cooking and laundry. This offspring requires five wake-up calls every morning.

D. Offspring lives away from home, sharing a clean apartment with a friend. Both have good jobs and cars. They fulfill all their own daily needs. But they spend every free moment they have at home with their family.

E. Nester has a job, a car and insurance, helps around the house, pays room and board to his parents, and gets along well with other family members. Offspring asks parents for advice but makes own decisions.

Answers

"**A**" shouts dependency by only sporadically paying his way at home, sleeping late, not getting along with family members, nor helping with household chores, and thus should be graded as a "2."

"**B**" shows independence in being able to support himself in his own apartment with a good job and car, but shows immaturity by living in a pigsty and needing to use his parents' laundry facilities, and so merits an "8."

"**C**" indicates independence in contributing income and helping with chores, but shows dependency in needing to have five calls to get up in the morning, and consequently is given a "9."

"**D**" portrays independence in apartment living, job and transportation, but shows some dependence on her family for needing to spend so much time with them, also resulting in an "8."

"**E**" is certainly an independent, mature person, even though he lives at home, and is therefore awarded a "10."

Your grading decisions may differ, but reading the quiz and making a decision regarding maturity will be helpful in seeing varying degrees of maturity in nesters.

Most adult offspring view themselves as independent when they move out of the parental home. Are they really independent, though, if they continue to rely on parents for money, emotional support, or other daily needs like food, and clean clothes? On the other hand, is it necessarily true that an adult offspring living at home is dependent, especially if he or she is exhibiting all the characteristics of an independent person?

Nesters are in transition from dependence to independence. Transitions are hard for all of us. Some offspring have a more difficult time accomplishing this feat.

Parents need patience at this time. However, if parents would look back at their own lives, most would probably recall that the transition from youth to adulthood was one of their most difficult times.

Helping nesters become independent

To aid the transition, there are some concrete things that parents can consider:

See your nesters as adults. Parents need to view their nesters as adults, as capable and responsible individuals. Even if they aren't, do not insist on giving.

Release your authority and keep your advice to yourself in order to support them in the transition to independence. Assuredly, it's difficult for a parent to visualize his or her child as an adult. Syndicated columnist Sydney Harris tells why this is so. He feels he can't be rational about the fact that his children have grown up because he loves his children, and how can love be rational? Here's Harris' column on the subject:

Are parents rational about their children? No. Parents aren't rational because love isn't rational. Young people can recognize this about romantic love, but they find it hard to accept the same fierce element in parental affection.

What brings this up was my eldest daughter's question the other day. "Let me ask you something, dad," she began, in a tone of patiently controlled exasperation that every experienced parent is familiar with.

"I sailed around the Mediterranean in a schooner when I was 17," she recited slowly and carefully. "I hiked through the Pyrenees from Spain to Paris. I've done rock climbing and deep-sea diving and slept in rain forests in the jungle of Indonesia. Right?"

"Right," I said, shivering at this recital, as a man would who gets hysterical while taking a shower if a bit of soap stings his eye. "So what?"

"So this," she went on. "When I'm home, and I'm going to the corner drugstore to pick up a shampoo, why do you always tell me to be careful how I cross the street?"

There is no satisfactory answer a parent can give to this.

All I could mumble in response was that when I was a man of 50, my mother would lean out of the window when I left and remind me not to drive too fast. If I were 80, and she were still alive, I would be getting the same admonition. No matter the age, a child is a child.

There is another factor, too, that children find it hard to understand. When they are far away, there is nothing we can do about their safety or welfare. They are in the hands of the gods. Parents try not to think about it, hoping that by blotting it out, the fateful call or cable will never come.

But when they are close by again, the old protective urge quickly reasserts itself, and it matters not how far they have been or how long gone, or even how well they have demonstrated their survival ability.

Most accidents, after all, happen around the corner, not in the rain forest. Man is a more dangerous foe to man than the elements of nature or animals in the wild. The most instinctive act of nearly every creature is to protect its young, and with humans this response persists a lifetime.

In the parent's mind, a child grows, but does not age. Rational?

No. But if we were wholly rational, would we want children at all?[16]

Harris feels that if children live away from home and are out of sight, then parents don't worry about them so much. However, when they come back to roost, their parents may once again become protective, and start giving unsolicited advice.

Married couples who are nesters complain of having to be answerable to parental authority, even though they have reached adulthood years ago. One couple says they are having severe problems with the wife's father, with whom they are living, because he insists upon waiting up until they come home at night. "My dad just won't go to sleep until he hears us at the door," complained the wife/daughter. "According to my parents, we never really grew up," she says.[17]

So, we can see how it is difficult at times for nesters to be considered adults by their parents. What a handicap for the nester in his growth toward independence. But what a challenge for both nesters and parents to make it happen!

Don't insist on giving. Untieing the apron strings is particularly difficult for children whose parents insist on giving. Giving can come in many forms: money, cars, room and board, or words of wisdom.

By giving nesters too much, parents can make them think that these things come easy in the real world. This, of course, is not true! Thus parents are misleading their offspring. It's very tempting for nesters to accept a gift, but the young adult has to take responsibility for not being seduced, especially if the parent is easily hurt by refusal of the gift. It's not always a simple matter for an offspring to say, "Thanks, but no thanks."[18]

Howard Halpern, a psychologist and popular author, gives us a further insight. "Every parent has two parts, an inner child and a mature parent. The mature parenting part really wants to launch the child and when that part is dominant, gifts can be given with no strings attached. But the inner child part of the parent may need to cling, fearing abandonment by the offspring and if that part of the parent is dominant, a gift may be intended to control." He states that some parents unconsciously want to keep their grown children dependent and close to them.[19]

In a way, they attempt to bribe their children into staying with them, or at least into being dependent on them. So if you want to help your children on the road to independence, you may want to analyze your gift-giving patterns.

Release your authority. Parents must realize that their task of child rearing is finished when their offspring reach adulthood.

Dr. Roberta Chaplan, a New York psychologist, says that a young, dependent child should accept authority from the parent, but that an adult should ultimately become his or her own authority.[20] For example, when children are small, they do what they are told by their parents, but when they become adults, they make their own decisions and take responsibility for the consequences of the ensuing actions.

The following poem, written decades ago, encourages a mother to release her hold over her grown son.

To the Mother of a Young Son

Hold your breath but not his hand
When he climbs to the top of the tree.
You can't go, too—the journey's his.
There's a lot of world to see.

He found a haven in your arms,
But now he's on his own,
The track is there and he must run.
And he must run alone.

The cord was cut when you gave him birth—
They placed him near your heart.
Yours to guide, yours to love
And yours to watch depart.

— Shirley Taylor Lambert [21]

Nesters are adults in the process of becoming their own authority on concerns in their own lives. They especially don't want to be subservient to others after reaching adulthood. So, parents need to let go of the strings and release their parental authority.

In other words, there has to be a shift for the parent from the authority figure to equality as an adult. This is a freeing action, in and of itself. It releases your adult offspring and enables him or her to grow. Parents can still pass on their experiences after their children become adults. But now they must share it as loving teachers, and no longer as authority figures.[22]

Keep Your Advice to Yourself. Parental advice: keep it, unless you're asked for it. While maintaining a keen interest in our nesters' lives, we parents have to resist the temptation to try to manage our grown children's lives. Some parents have a difficult time relinquishing their role as advice givers, but it's important to learn to give advice without coercing, to disagree without provoking guilt, and to allow freedom, while at the same time pointing out dangers and pitfalls.[23]

One nester complains that her parents are still trying to run her life. But what she doesn't seem to realize is that she continues to discuss every aspect of her life with them. By giving her parents so many details, she is implying that she really wants their advice.[24]

Nesters need to realize that if they take responsibility for their own actions, their parents can relax and often will allow the nesters to take care of themselves. If the offspring aren't taking responsibility, it's time for an in-depth family discussion.

Jory Graham, whose syndicated newspaper column "Time for Living" deals with cancer patients, wrote an article which was especially applicable to this topic of how parents and families can help nesters become independent. Graham wrote that the help that is needed by cancer patients is the kind that encourages efforts to become independent. They need this encouragement just as much as they need to be quietly listened to as they share some of their deepest feelings.

She could just as easily have been voicing the thoughts of adult offspring struggling to become independent. "Each time you (parents) usurp our fundamental right to make our own decisions and our own mistakes, you become more of a problem to us than a help. That's when we become resentful and unappreciative. If the time comes that we need help, we'll let you know."[25]

Parents must learn when to help and when to let grown children help themselves. That's not easy for parents, but that's what is needed. A study[26] by the national research firm of Yankelovich, Skelly and White, shows that younger parents are rather self-oriented, while older, more traditional parents are likely to sacrifice for their children.

So, older, traditional parents must be especially alert to a tendency to do things for their offspring. It will be harder for these parents to allow their offspring to become independent.

A few questions will help you analyze whether your nester really wants advice or help from you. When your nester tells you about a problem, you can ask: "Can you handle this yourself? Do you want some advice on how to solve it? Do you need help solving it? Or do you just want me to listen?"

In this way, you are shifting the responsibility and the decision-making to your nester. You can also determine whether your nester wants to dump the problem on you (which you could transfer back to him or her) or whether he or she really needs advice or actually needs help in solving the problem.

Erma Bombeck, in a column entitled, *"Kids grow up only when their parents permit it,"* allows us see the humor of our offspring becoming independent. Erma writes that parents say, "You have to learn to live with your own mistakes." Yet, in the next breath we find ourselves saying things like, "Look, Daddy and I will pay to have your car repaired and you can pay us back later."

Another example she used was a mother saying, "It's time you were responsible for yourself." But then adding, "I've made a dental appointment for you Tuesday and picked up your cleaning."[27]

If we want our nesters to act maturely, we can't keep treating them like children. We need to remember that it helps our nesters to act in a mature manner if we see them as adults.

Maturity and independence

Nesters have many ways to show that they are independent. They can make their own decisions and take responsibility for them, they can pay their own way, they can take care of their daily needs, and they can be emotionally stable. We'll look at specific instances in which nesters can exemplify maturity and independence.

Make decisions and take the responsibility for them. One of the criteria of independence is being able to make decisions, and feel confident about those decisions, without having to seek approval. If a nester is able to look at a problem from all angles, weigh the consequences of a decision, and then go ahead and decide, fully accepting all the consequences, he or she is certainly fulfilling one of the criteria of being an independent person. One cannot feel really independent unless he or she is comfortable with the decisions he or she makes.

One mother of two nesters, a son 21 and a daughter 20, says that she encourages her nesters to solve their own problems and make their own decisions. When her daughter needed to get the brakes repaired on her car, she decided on a repair shop herself. This meant checking out various places or people who fixed brakes and then determining where she could get the best quality work for the least amount of money. By solving this problem, she was able to grow more toward being independent.

Family counselor Oscar Christensen states, "By letting children live with their decisions, parents encourage the development of self-reliance, preparing the child for his ultimate departure from the house, which is the goal of all parenting."[28]

One young man had difficulty in this realm. He had a penchant for driving the sporty new car his parents had given him much too fast. Each time he was stopped for speeding, his parents would come to the rescue. They paid his tickets, and also paid his auto insurance when he went on risk status at a much higher rate.

This young man was not able to learn from his wrongdoing because his parents rescued him from the consequences. It is going to be more difficult for this young adult to mature because he didn't learn from his mistakes.

Sister Kathleen Bierne, a family education coordinator, feels that parents should "allow the child to live with consequences. The temptation to protect from error and rescue immediately is strong in those who are involved in the relationship of parenting. Unless real danger is involved, or circumstances change the original intent of the decision, try to avoid doing both, protecting and rescuing. It is essential that without abandoning or moralizing, the parent stands beside the offspring and reassures him or her that the decision can be lived with in a positive way."[29]

Pay your way. One parent felt that nesters paying their own way, especially rent and utilities, is necessary for young adults to prove that they are independent.[30] To be considered independent in our society, where one can't get along without money, means the ability to pay to house, feed, clothe, insure, transport, entertain and clean yourself. The list could go on and on. The nesters' budget will tell them how much can be spent in each area.

Take care of your daily needs. One parent, a mother of three nesters ages 25, 20 and 18, said that she felt that accepting and assuming the responsibilities of life was a real sign of independence. She felt that if nesters were able to care for their own daily needs, they would be well on the road to being self-sufficient. And, this includes a multitude of daily, routine things that sometimes elude us, such as are found in the next table, *Daily chores.*

Daily chores

keep living space clean	*plan menus*
wash clothes	*buy food*
iron clothes	*prepare food*
mend clothes	*wash dishes*
balance checkbook	*type papers*
prepare income tax materials	*take care of car or bike*
file important papers	*undertake repair jobs*
plan a budget	*get to work on time*

One father complained to a counselor that he was having trouble getting his son up in time for work. The following conversation ensued:

Counselor: "Tell me what happens on an average workday."
Dad: "I have to call and call my son, sometimes as many as ten times, in order to finally get him out of bed! By the time he does get up, I'm so angry that I can barely be civil toward him."
Counselor: "How old is your son?"
Dad: "24."
Counselor: "Why do you still feel getting him up is your responsibility?"
Dad: "If I don't get him up, then he's late for work. If that happens too often, then I'm afraid he'll lose his job."
Counselor: "If you want to do something for your son, you can get him an alarm clock."
Dad: "We've tried that, but he just sleeps through the alarm."
Counselor: "At 24, he should be getting himself up, managing his own time."
Dad: "But I don't want to see him lose his job!"
Counselor: "How long are you going to go on being responsible for your son's time? All his life? Sooner or later he's going to have to learn how to get to work by himself. Wouldn't it be better sooner

than later? Now, he probably has an entry-level position; later, he may have a more important job and be living on his own. Would you like to see him lose that job because of tardiness? Let your son be responsible for his own time now, and let him suffer the consequences of his own actions. Let him realize that if he doesn't get to work on time, he may lose a job. Some people have to learn through mistakes."

A widow had her three grown sons living with her. She was grateful for her sons' company and glad that they stayed home. However, as the months went on she became resentful toward them because she felt that they were using her. They came to expect home-cooked meals, fresh clothes and a clean home—all at no cost to them!

She asked in a variety of ways for them to contribute money, help shop, or lend a hand with household chores. All to no avail. They reasoned that Mom didn't need the money (Dad had left her well off), she had time to shop (it gave her something to do) and what self-respecting guy wanted to vacuum anyway?

Finally, in desperation, Mom rented an apartment, leaving them to fend for themselves. Fortunately, she was financially able to abandon the investment she had in her home. She then deeded the house over to the sons as part of their inheritance. Now she found time to arrange her widowhood so that it became a time of healing and new growth for her. She still sees her sons frequently, but she's no longer their personal maid.

This is not to say that all nesters should be able to do all these things on their own. They should be able to take care of themselves or decide who can help them with the things that they can't do. Tax forms don't get filed automatically and flat tires can't be ignored.

Be stable emotionally. Emotional stability is a good sign of a mature, independent person, and especially important in the relationships we have with family, friends and co-workers. When relating to family members, mature nesters treat family with care, concern and respect. If nesters tend to treat friends better than family, it is a sign of immaturity. It would be a sign of immaturity to refuse to accept help from other family members during a negative mood or depression.

Keeping feelings inside causes us to lose our perspective. Unchecked depression, sarcasm, or moodiness spreads like wildfire in close living quarters, and nesters need to be able to control these emotions and to accept help in dealing with them.

A mother was having difficulty with her 19-year-old daughter. The daughter was acting irresponsibly—not working, not going to school, partying and indulging in excessive sleeping. One day, Mom called her former husband to tell him that when she awoke that morning both her daughter and her car were gone. Now, she had just received a frantic phone call from the daughter, saying that she was out of money and the car was out of gas. She needed someone to come and get her. The mother asked the former husband if he could go and fetch her. This he did, realizing it was time for professional counseling. He felt these rescues just couldn't continue. When asked what the problem was, he replied, "She's acting like a 12-year-old."

"What happened when she was 12 years old?" questioned the counselor. The startled father replied, "Why that's when her mother and I got divorced!" Often emotional growth will stop when a child receives a traumatic shock. The divorce was just such a shock for this daughter. She needed counseling, even six years after the event. She was fixated at that point in her life and could not proceed until she accepted the divorce. Only then was she able to deal with it and get on with her life.

A word of caution is needed here. When a nester is emotionally unstable, mental illness may be present that will require professional help and possibly a stay in an institution, not only for the nester's safety but the safety of others.

One mother is still trying to get over the shock of learning that her 20-year-old son, while living in her home, abducted, molested and killed an 8-year-old girl, tormenting her for 36 hours. The son hid the little girl in his mother's basement for more than 24 hours without, of course, the mother, her second husband, or her visiting daughter being aware of the child's presence.

The son graduated from high school with straight A's and was a member of the National Honor Society. He went on to college and held a full-time job as an assistant manager at a restaurant, but complained that the job was beneath him. He told people that he was going to be a university professor. Soon he complained that his job was cutting into his schooling. Finally he quit his job, with no other in sight. Then, for a short while he sold fire extinguishers. He didn't manage what little money he had very well, buying, among other items, a large color television and a compact disc player, all beyond his means. He had to drop out of the university because of lack of funds. Then he was out of school and out of a job as well. He eventually obtained a full-time job at a discount variety store. At this point, his mother relaxed, feeling that her son was getting his life together. But very quickly he again complained about his work.

Allegedly, this young man told the police that he killed the child because he was bored. He'd been plotting to abduct and kill someone for quite awhile. Where did this young man go wrong? A friend recalled the many hours they'd spent together playing an occult fantasy adventure game.

Later, the police found books about occultism, demons, wizards, astrology and witchcraft, as well as almost 100 pornography magazines in his room. A friend described the murderer as moderate to very depressed. His co-workers called him "The Ogre" because he could be a grouch. Now his mother wonders if this tragedy have been avoided by early treatment. Meanwhile the alleged murderer's lawyer is planning to use mental illness as a defense.[31]

In another tragic instance, a couple had a 25-year-old son, John, who suffered from bouts of what was thought to be depression and immaturity. In reality, John's problem was mental illness. His mother felt that John needed professional help; however, a psychiatrist simply suggested that he be kicked out of the parental home so that he'd be forced to learn to become independent. This advice backfired when John shot then-President Ronald Reagan.

What John Hinckley really needed was the proper treatment, most probably early in his life. As in Hinckley's case, there are definite warning signs that can alert parents when and if their nester may be mentally ill.

Psychiatrists say that when the following signs are pronounced, persistent, recurring, and/or progressive, a nester (or any other person) may be dealing with mental illness. These signs are: confused thinking; obsessions; compulsions and uncontrollable urges; inability to cope with everyday life; difficulty with friendships; a pattern of failure; prolonged or severe depression; immaturity; atypical physical illnesses; either neglect of or exaggerated concern for personal hygiene; difficulty adjusting to change; undue anxiety; too little or too much sleep; excessive self-centeredness; rapid weight fluctuation; either no emotional responses or exaggerated responses; negative self-image; frequent changes of plans; either extreme aggressiveness or exaggerated docility; listlessness.

Psychiatrists tell us that mentally ill persons may look and act normal much of the time. Mental illness has many causes, but it is not caused by normal parental behavior. Mental illness "strikes one in five adults, one in three families... Whatever the provocation, don't throw the ill person out of the home. Telling him 'you're on your own' only increases pressures the sick person has already found too much to handle."[32]

Don't just throw the sick person out. Get help if he or she needs it. Many mentally ill individuals achieve full recovery.

Does nesting foster or hinder independence?

In the view of author Jay Haley, there's nothing wrong with the offspring who chooses to live at home. "Some people don't want to get married, and they stay with their parents until the parents get old, and then they care for them. If these offspring are working and doing something productive with their lives, it's perfectly reasonable. It's when someone stays at home and is chronically inadequate, always failing—and the parents always worrying about them and taking care of them—then it's pathological."[33]

There seems to be no clear-cut answer to the above question of whether nesting fosters or hinders independence. Parents in my survey had differing views on this subject. Some parents who responded to the questionnaires were adamant in their belief that nesting fosters growth, and other parents were just as resolute that it hindered growth! Perhaps the answer is as individual as each of us.

It's interesting to note the comments of those who believe that nesting fosters independence:

One 22-year-old woman wrote, "My parents have never put any obstacles in the way of my own decision-making."

A mother of a 28-year-old man who is a teacher says, "He is thoroughly a responsible person. He's always done more than we ask of him and he does it on his own."

A father writes that his son, who is 22, working and going to school, lives in a room off their recreation area. "It's far enough removed so that his coming and going is relatively unnoticed. As he attends school and works as well, he is seldom at home." This son appears to live a life quite independent of his parents, even though they share the same house.

A mother of three adult offspring comments: "When they can make it on their own, they'll leave—all three of my children have finally left. I can't really believe that my adult children run the risk of stagnating when living at home. It seems to me that a great many young people's problems are directly related to being on their own. They have complete freedom and tend to try drugs, alcohol, and sex because they have no one to make them feel guilty about abusing these things."

"Living at home gives offspring a good, secure background to use as a springboard when facing the world," says one mom. "Yes, our 31-year-old nesting daughter accepts the responsibilities of life. Yes, she helps around the house. She is part of our family! It also helps her career. You see, she is contemplating a job shift, away from the teaching profession. Because she is living at home, she is able to do some researching into different fields. We certainly recognize her as an adult—she's been an independent adult for over 10 years. She has her own space and really only shares the conveniences of kitchen and laundry. She is decidedly a boarder and we have very little trouble with this. For seven years she was a very responsible, independent single person living and working away from home."

"Both of our grown children who are living at home are independent enough. They take care of themselves."

"I feel that having adult offspring living at home fosters their growth in four areas—responsibility, career, social life and serious love relationship."

"Commitment, self-control and self-discipline are often lacking in the growing process outside the family atmosphere. It's better for them to live at home."

"Our son takes responsibility for his actions. He seems to get along socially. Living at home provides a home base for job seeking. Serious love relationship? Living at home helps to provide a family setting for accepting the girlfriend. If parents are responsible, children seem to follow suit."

One of the benefits that some parents felt accompanied living at home was that their offspring didn't have to rush into, or cling to, a love relationship. They were getting plenty of normal family love.

The following story is a prime example of one father who enjoyed living, working and just being with his children—both when they were young and as they grew older. His grown children learned many skills while living at home, which helped them become independent. This father felt that, if there was no reason for them to stay, his children would leave home. So, he planned one project after another to keep their interest.

"Looking back," he wrote, "I can see that I spent most of my parenting years trying to avoid the day when any of the children would leave home." His family lived in a small country home that had a barn. So he got horses that needed to be fed, ridden, cleaned and housed. They had a fireplace that needed wood which had to be sawed, chopped, carried and fires tended. They lived on the coast of Maine, and they had boats that had to be hauled, caulked and painted. They reaped the benefits of the sea—clams and eels. After that, the family turned to real estate. They bought and renovated old houses, barns and "woebegone buildings." They cleared trees, repaired, painted, sawed and shingled houses. Their labor force grew during the summers until it numbered as high as 60, including friends and neighbors who wanted to work to earn some money. "Finally, though, we ran out of needs and the children began to leave. Without needs there was no keeping the young." He envied those farmers who were able to keep their sons and daughters—they had the home place to work for their entire lives![34]

The offspring in that family were exposed to a wide variety of experiences which will ultimately help them lead independent lives. Surely, the children learned a great deal and grew in family closeness while they lived at home.

One mother felt that growth toward independence and maturity was very individual. She said that they raised four sons, all now over 18 years. Noticeable growth and independence was different for each one. Two were very mature at 18, but the other two were far from mature at that age. Therefore, she felt that parents needed to observe each child individually to recognize their particular needs and respond to them, whether this meant living at home or outside the home.

Following are comments by grown sons and daughters who feel that living at home helps them in their growth:

"I don't feel that living at home should adversely affect growth. One should have responsibilities even if one is living at home," says Barb, a 19-year-old nester.

"Living at home while attending school in town did not in any way hinder my adjustment to living away from home when I decided to go out of town to continue my education. There just doesn't seem to be much difference. I plan to continue living at home after graduation until I either marry, relocate, or buy my own home," relates a 24-year-old male nester.

"I am home because it is a way to save some money right now. And, you know, I still have my independence!" says a 26-year-old son.

"It shouldn't affect the growth of independence," writes a 22-year-old son at home.

"We function well as two independent units living together in the same house. I believe mine is a rather unique situation because I have lived independently away from home for five years (she is now 31). I've always been prepared for responsibility and independence. None of my time at home has been at my parents' expense financially. I love to be with my family. I can see how family love grows when I'm living at home."

"There are too many outside factors that still force people to grow, such as relationships with co-workers and peers and having to be out in the work place. I think comfortable is a better word than stagnation. I'm not the type who likes a lot of change in my life. Since my parents and I get along and there's nothing wrong with where I am, why go through the bother of moving?"

On the other hand, some people feel that nesting really does hinder growth. The following are comments from families with this view:

"Some grown kids sponge off their folks and take advantage of them. We know one family where the man is retired and his wife works hard as a waitress. They have a 37-year-old son who is home collecting unemployment. He thinks that these parents are, in effect, saying, 'Go ahead, take advantage of us.'"[35]

"I really think a child has to move out in order to grow up," one father relates.

"It makes me mad when I think of my sister spending all her money on clothes and living off our folks!" says an older brother of a nester. "She gets all the breaks."

What about those nesters who seem to be stagnating? Some parents feel that an adult offspring living at home risks role stagnation. They feel these nesters are surrounded by the environment of childhood and that makes it difficult for them to grow and move into a new adult role.

One woman writes about a relative of hers, whom she feels fell into this type of stagnation. This male relative, after his return home from World War II, lived with his parents until his father's death about 20 years ago. He continued to care for his mother for an additional five years, until she had to be placed in a nursing home, where she died. Following her death, he required counseling to cope with his guilt for placing her in a nursing home. Then, he had a series of girlfriends for about 10 years, but refused to get married. The relative relating the story says, "Going home again for a brief time may be the answer sometimes, but in the long run it may not enable one to develop a true sense of independence. Mother made her nest as cozy as possible and then reaped her reward in her old age, but at what cost to her son?"

One magazine article stated that a few young adults "risk permanent grounding because of emotional dependency. 'I came home mostly for economic reasons,' sighs Ed, an unemployed political science graduate who has lived with his parents in Boston for the past five years, 'but I never got out.'"[36]

Psychiatrist Paul Kingsley wonders if we are doing our young adults a favor by letting them stay on more or less permanently at home. Are we stifling their growth? Perhaps he had in mind someone like the above sons who were so deeply attached to their parents' home. This may be something that families should watch out for—an overdependence of the nester upon the family.

One nester, no longer young at 38, has lived with his parents as an adult since he was 24. He feels it hindered his development in all areas of his life. Yet he writes that his parents recognize him as an adult, encourage him to solve his own problems, make his own decisions and don't volunteer advice regarding his clothes, hair and general appearance. But still, he feels that an adult offspring who lives at home definitely risks role stagnation! Apparently he is stuck in the nesting role and can't force himself out it.

Roberta Chaplan, a New York psychiatrist, claims a "child should learn to accept authority and as an adult eventually become his or her own authority. In some cases, that step is never taken and the children continue to rely on parents' rules and not on their own. In a crisis situation especially, or when a big decision must be made, they listen to other people instead of trusting their own judgment."[37]

Why do these nesters react thus? Apparently, they have become so used to having their parents make decisions for them, they become unable to make decisions on their own. This is another area in which nesting families should be alert to possible negative developments.

One article states that for many adults a thread of dependency still ties them to their parents. "For some, this means being unable to make important decisions on their own. For others, it means being afraid to tell their parents how they feel about many things, and for still others it means continuing to look for ways to win the love and praise they enjoyed, or missed, as children.... Psychologists also say that many adults harbor fears from childhood that if they act in a way their parents disapprove of, the parents will abandon them or stop loving them."[38] A dangerous side effect to dependency is resentment.

One man, a 30-year-old writer, claimed his mother encouraged him to be dependent on her. "She never had a career and she needed to feel needed. One way to fulfill her needs was to take care of me. I guess I was so angry at myself for being in the position of feeling obliged to her that it came out in resentment towards her."[39] If parents are aware of this possible long-range effect, perhaps this feeling of dependency can be avoided.

Some offspring are caught in role stagnation—inability to grow into independence—because of a crisis in their middle-aged parents' lives. The National Institutes of Health conducted a study on 30 families with offspring entering adulthood. The offspring, because they were just getting started in life, had various options open in areas of work and love. Seeing this, many fathers seemed to regret the choices that they made in their own lives. Meanwhile, the mothers faced the prospect of an empty nest, with loss of their motherly role, as the offspring spoke of moving on. Thus, many of these mothers turned to their husbands for reinforcement of their own self-esteem. The husbands, however, were too wrapped up in regretting their own life choices and results to notice their wives' needs.

After being rejected by their husbands, most of the wives reacted by turning back to their children. This motherly concentration upon their children's lives made it difficult for them to take the steps needed to launch out on their own. Often the result was a resigned father, an intrusive mother and an abrupt and bitter exit by the offspring. Those offspring who remained at home had conflict, generally with their mother. In many of these 30 families, the offspring couldn't gain independence, form solid friendships or obtain a job.[40]

Author Jay Haley feels that there is an identifiable reason why some young people are constantly getting into trouble, via drugs, crime, or paralyzing apathy—because of a need on the part of these offspring to preserve the family. These young people do this by sacrificing their own growth. The offspring's failure prevents parents from facing issues in their marriage that might lead to divorce. The offspring keep the parents concentrating on their problems to the neglect of the offspring's own problems. The price that is paid is the lack of emotional growth in the offspring. These young people, either consciously or subconsciously, refuse to succeed in their growth toward independence. Often they are not able to function in school, work or close friendships. Some offspring fail just before the point of success—right before graduation, failing to find a job, losing one job after another, or taking menial jobs below their capabilities.[41]

The above type of offspring, as described by Haley, certainly is stuck in the rut of role stagnation. If parents were aware of this syndrome and recognized it in their own situation, possibly they would be motivated to take care of their marriage problems. Likely, the marriage would either improve or dissolve. In either case, this would allow the young adult to grow at a regular pace.

Growth or stagnation

Becoming independent entails many actions on the part of the nester and parents. It is an easy, gradual progress for some; it's a harder road for others. Nesting may foster or hinder growth toward independence depending on how parents and nesters act. If, however, families are aware of pitfalls, nesting can be a growing experience.

Marlin

CHAPTER SIX

Communications:
so let's talk about it

"A happy family is but an earlier heaven."
— Sir John Bowring, a 19th century diplomat,
writer and linguist [1]

Many young people living at home are in a state of transition or growth, which can cause pressure and tension for both parents and offspring. In turn, this pressure and tension can make communications difficult. Sometimes the nesting situation requires the wisdom of Solomon, the patience of Job and the kindness of a saint—from the parents as well as the nester. The secret of living agreeably with adult children, or anybody, is communication. This chapter will cover various types of communications. It will also deal with specific topics relating to nesting that need open communications between nesting family members.

Communicating in anger—healed with love

Hidden resentment can be the real problem behind blocked communications. Sometimes the only way to get hidden resentment out in the open is by direct conflict. Even though this may be distasteful, it sometimes is necessary to clear the air, especially if there is long-standing resentment. The following example touchingly illustrates this problem and then shows how love was able to restore the relationship.

This family had two adult daughters, 24 and 19, living at home. In addition, they had a son, 23, and another daughter, 10. When they were growing up, the two elder daughters shared a bedroom; bad feelings developed about the neatness of the room, sharing of clothes and when to turn off the light. They continuously had trouble getting along with each other; their yelling and screaming were incessant. It was adversely affecting the entire family. This bad blood was never resolved. It alternately surfaced and subsided, but never really went away.

The parents knew that matters between the two were not getting better, and, in fact, were getting worse. One Sunday evening, the parents returned home from a day-long church seminar to hear yet another fight in progress. Mom's heart had not been in the seminar that day because she was very concerned about the two daughters. She had taken that opportunity to pray that God would somehow help them get along better. As the day wore on, her burden seemed heavier. By 5 p.m. she felt extremely concerned about having left them alone for so many hours. As she and her husband drove home, her shoulders drooped and she was fearful of what they'd find upon their arrival. Even the sun had abandoned them, she thought, as thunder clouds began to gather.

The minute the parents opened the front door, they were greeted by the youngest daughter tattling that her two older sisters had been fighting all day. Mom wondered how bad it had been and immediately felt guilty for having left them. The parents, son and younger daughter all converged upon the combatants, who now were shouting at each other at the bottom of the basement steps. The two eldest daughters screamed at each other with an intensity that Mom had never heard before. Mom cannot now recall the cause—and the daughters probably don't either—but it was a vicious argument! Mom sank helplessly onto the bottom basement step in despair, staring at the knotty pine walls, seeing a recreation room where happy family times were supposed to occur.

Her thoughts drifted back to another argument the daughters had told her about. That time, the two girls had been arguing so violently that one had picked up an ottoman and threatened to smash her sister's skull. Her angry sister jeered, "Come on. I dare you. Come on. Kill me!" Later, the instigator told Mom she had really intended to harm her sister. Fortunately, her sister's boyfriend was present and he stepped between them, disarming the attacker.

"When, oh when, Lord, would there ever be peace between these two sisters?" Mom prayed. It seemed as though all the years she had poured into mothering were for naught.

Then a touching thing happened: the son began to weep softly. He was overcome with great sadness at seeing his two sisters screaming hatred back and forth. Very quickly, the son's weeping turned to great heaving sobs which racked his whole body uncontrollably. His fighting sisters could no longer ignore him. They turned to their brother in an attempt to console him. But he was unable to stop and could not even talk, so great was his emotion.

It was obvious to the girls how deeply they were hurting him. They tried to console their brother, but nothing seemed to help. One begged, "What can we do to make you stop crying?" But he was unable to reply, so they could only hug him. Finally, they encircled him with their arms, spoke soothingly and begged him to stop crying. The brother, in turn, put his arms around both sisters and pulled them together. He loved each of them and they each loved him, if not each other. Soon, the two girls were apologizing to each other. The younger sister ran to get hankies for the family, for everyone was in tears.

Over a decade has gone by since that tumultuous day. These two daughters have had disagreements since, but the bitter, deep-rooted and long-standing resentment between the two seems to be gone. They can now talk over their differences as they arise without building up resentments that used to turn into violent fights.

Using body language in communication

The family which can identify body language can relate better to the emotional states of one another. If a family can't get problems out in the open, things just get worse.

Let's look at Kim. She was angry with her mother, because Kim thought her parents were spoiling the younger children. She felt that they were being treated better than she had been treated when she was younger. Janie, her little sister, has just gotten a new bicycle, and Kim remembers how she had been given a second-hand one years ago when she was Janie's age. But Kim couldn't talk about it. So one day she didn't say good-bye before she left for work. Mother felt hurt at this obvious omission and in the back of her mind she knew that this was a red flag. Something was bothering Kim.

The next morning Kim not only neglected to say goodbye, but she slammed the door as well. Matters weren't resolved that evening either, and the following morning Kim slammed the door so hard the window next to the front door shattered! Kim was not able to verbalize her anger, but she was saying loud and clear, "Hey, something you did bothers me!" By reading Kim's body language and responding to it, this mother could have used a shortcut in their communications and saved a window. She could have talked it out with Kim and found out what was bothering her. Then she could have said, "I'm sorry you feel we are playing favorites. But we have more money now than we did when you were little. We help you now in other ways. We did the best we could for you when you were young, according to our income then."

We can use body language to help us get along with our nesters by realizing that we act out our state of being with non-verbal language, says author Julian Fast. "We lift one eyebrow for disbelief. We rub our noses with puzzlement. We clasp our arms to isolate ourselves or to protect ourselves. We shrug our shoulders for indifference, wink one eye for intimacy, tap our fingers for impatience, slap our forehead for forgetfulness."[2]

The quickest and plainest kind of body language is touch. "The touch of a hand, or an arm around someone's shoulder, can send a more vivid and direct message than dozens of words."[3]

Psychiatrist Hugh Riordan urges families to touch. "Try family back rubs," he urges. This helps loosen us up and gets the talk flowing. Lightly touch a child as you walk by or put your hand on an arm as you talk. This shows that you really care about the person you touch.

To encourage a nester to talk, the parent can sit, stoop, or slope his or her body. This shows empathy and will put a grown son or daughter on a more even footing with the parent.[4]

If during a heated discussion, you realize that the other person is sending some messages, swinging a leg or tapping a finger, this is a clue that he is getting ready to leave. It's time to try to remove or lessen the tension, if you want to continue to talk.

Drawn-in shoulders, Julius Fast says, mean that the person is having suppressed anger; raised shoulders mean fear; squared shoulders mean that he is shouldering some responsibility, and bowed shoulders mean that he is carrying a burden or a heavy load. A person with arms and legs crossed is saying that he feels a tightness and is withdrawn. Asking that person to uncross his legs and arms may help him open up and talk.[5]

By reading body language, we can get the talk flowing, bring out hidden resentments, and have a happier life with our nester. Communicating effectively, with whatever means at hand, including body language, is a worthy goal.

Negotiation and compromise

Negotiation and compromise are also communication tools you should consider using. Ralph Ranieri, a family counselor, suggests that families start with negotiation in solving problems.[6]

Start by listing problems. Then brainstorm for possible solutions. Others are not invited to criticize the proposed solutions. The family can then address any objections. Often a consensus is reached during this negotiation process. "When the whole family gets into the act of negotiating," Ranieri states, "some very productive decision-making can go on." If negotiation fails, then the family can turn to compromise. In compromising, each side gives up a little in order to reach an agreement.

Listening

When nesters are deeply troubled, be it a personal situation or something relating to a troubled friend, it often helps if a parent listens. At this point, direction and counsel are not requested or desirable, but a sounding board will help lighten the burden. Sorrow shared is sorrow halved.

One mother writes that her three daughters needed this type of help. Neither of her two sons required or wanted this intimacy, but for some reason, the daughters did. The daughters seemed to be able to open up late at night, but unfortunately Mom was a morning person. She compromised by inviting them into the parental bedroom, after Dad was deep in slumber, for late night chats. It was hard to stay awake, Mom says, but oh, so rewarding. She felt so privileged to be taken into her daughters' confidences, hopes and dreams that it made up for the effort to stay awake.

A second mom also wrote that often her daughter and two sons conversed in depth late at night after Dad was snoring away. This mom felt it was important to be interested, to listen and not to argue or give advice. These special times were sharing times—memory builders.

Pressures that nesters endure

Circumstantial pressures upon nesters may lead to a breakdown in inter-family communications. Where once nesters may have lived in harmony within the home when they were children, now that they are adults, problems may suddenly so intervene with responsibilities that open communications are in jeopardy.

Difficulty in communicating with parents, a failure grade at school or a problem at work could mean an impossible time for the whole family. Decisions about school, career and/or marriage that will affect them throughout their entire lives are generally made by an offspring while nesting. How these determinations are formulated can shape relationships between nesters and parents.

Nester Stephen Berg feels that the following points help him get along with his mom:

1. Grow up and act maturely.

2. Respect differences, realizing that everyone is entitled to his or her opinions and that your thoughts don't need to coincide.

3. Appreciate helpfulness, but don't expect it. Acknowledge a kindness, but don't feel it's your right.

4. Be patient. Problems require patience, and patience is an oppor tunity for growth.[7]

It's the small, meaningful acts we do that show others how much they mean to us.

School. John has decided to go on to college, but he can't decide which one. Application deadlines are near, the pressure is on for a decision. John is normally a loving, considerate family member, but because of these pressures, he becomes uncommunicative and irritable. Lately, a typical scene with John is as follows: It's been hours since John came home from school and no one has seen or heard from him since. Mother sends Sarah, a little sister, to find John and tell him that supper is ready. She finds John in his room, and in response to her invitation, he snarls, "Tell Mom I'm busy and can't eat for another hour!"

It is obvious that John needs some assistance in dealing with his college choice. A sympathetic parent can help alleviate some of his indecision by taking time to discuss with him what characteristics he should be considering when choosing a school. Some examples might be:

Size: Does he want a small, close-knit college atmosphere or a large and somewhat impersonal university setting?

Location: How far is it from home? Will the distance impair his ability to get home for vacations or long weekends? (Some freshmen and sophomores come home once a month on scheduled three-day weekends. Some schools lock up for these long weekends, forcing students to find a place to go.)

Public or parochial: Does he want to be on a secular campus or have the religious setting of a parochial school?

Curricula: Does the school have the courses and accreditation in the area he wants to study? If he is undecided, does the school have a wide variety of courses from which to choose? A variety of courses will help him narrow down his options for study.)

Cost: How much can he afford and how much can the parents afford to help him? (It is very important to discuss this, laying out clearly each party's responsibility. The student can't budget his finances if parents aren't explicit about their ability and willingness to help financially and in what amount. If parents are unable or unwilling to help out, they should inform their offspring of this fact.)

Financial aid: What about scholarships, grants and student loans? (These may be critical and all have deadlines that can sneak up on you.)

Type of school: College, university, two-year junior college or trade/vocational school? (Maybe a different type of school would satisfy the nester's requirements better than the school he thinks he wants to attend.)

In addition to these basic considerations, it may be helpful to go into depth on a few of the above items.

In view of inflation, we must plan for rising education costs. One private college estimates that, in 10 years, costs will quadruple. This may force nesters to remain living in their parents' home and commute to school to save money on room and board. Many families have stated that when their offspring commute it is more difficult for them to stay interested in school. When living on campus, students are drawn into extracurricular activities, and this seems to help them continue until graduation.

Some parents have their hearts set on college degrees for their children and are bitterly disappointed if they do not attend or complete college. But some students who attempt advanced schooling find it too difficult and are forced to drop out. Rick, a college sophomore, smashed his fist through a large glass window on campus out of sheer frustration over his failing grades. This resulted in serious personal injury and expulsion from college. In addition, the suicide rate of college students is on the increase.[8]

With this evidence, parents and nesters need to be honest with themselves and come to a decision on whether a degree is really desirable. The Bureau of Labor estimates that one out of every four college graduates will have to settle for a job beneath his or her expectations because there are more diplomas than the economy can support. Some college graduates feel that the time and money they expended on getting a degree was unnecessary.

From the statistics below, we can see that a significant percentage of people are entering the work force immediately after high school graduation. This does not mean, however, that they will not return to formal schooling later. After a year or two, they may decide to re-enroll.

- 57.9 percent of our high school graduates each year will go on to college.

- 39.6 percent will attempt to enter the job market on a full-time basis.[9]

In conclusion, nesters have a choice to make about a school or job. Help in this decision may be necessary, so talk about it!

If you do, everyone will feel better and know what to expect from each other. Even though there may be disappointment for parents if their child drops out of school or wants to attend a trade school instead of a four-year college, parents should realize that millions of other parents and nesters are suffering through the same choices and decisions. There is often an upward mobility from generation to generation. The children get more schooling and a better job than their fathers or mothers. But upward mobility is not always the case, and not always necessary.

Job hunting. This may be another pressure with which nesters have to grapple. If they have decided to enter the work field rather than continue a formal education, they may need help in deciding what they want to do and where they should look for work. Jobs are usually found through word of mouth, want ads, and private or governmental agencies. Emotional support is definitely needed for those who are job hunting. It is especially so when jobs are scarce. Job hunting can be a tedious, ego-deflating, and emotionally depressing experience. This is when nesters need an extra boost.

One father relates a clear and concise approach for helping a nester in the job hunt. He says, "We sometimes think that a young person can just go out and get a job. For many parents this was the case 40 years ago, but it is not always true today. However, he or she needs help and encouragement at a very early age with assistance in applying for jobs. It's never easy to make that first big step, and most children will resist every effort when you try to encourage them to get a job. They make remarks like, 'I am grown up and I can do this in my own time,' or 'I want to have my youth, I'm not ready to get a job yet,' or 'All you ever think about is getting me to go to work.'" Sometimes a job application form is overwhelming and the applicant's mind goes blank. The applicant could ask, "I'm too busy right now to fill this out. Can I take it with me and return it tomorrow?" Many companies will allow this.

The father continues: "The kids leave us, their parents, with terrible guilt feelings saying that we are pushing them out to work too soon. Yet, we know that what they are really saying is, 'I'm scared. What will the employer say to me? How much should I ask for in pay? What happens if he says no?'

"We, as parents, should be introducing our children, while they are young, to the fact that they will need to earn a living somehow. Perhaps as early as age 14, they should be applying for a part-time job. This will help them get used to prospective employers saying 'no,' and also hopefully know the satisfaction of an employer saying, 'Yes. When can you start?'"

Getting a variety of job experiences is extremely helpful in deciding what type of job or profession they might desire in the future. As parents, we have the responsibility of helping them through this stage of their lives. They need our input as to what their abilities and talents are—as we see them. This knowledge will help them when they need to consider a profession to fit their talents, skills and abilities.

When jobs are scarce, families may have to be creative in bringing in the needed finances. The following mother/son combination seems to have found a common solution for each of their problems. This family suffered through a divorce when the three children were between 8 and 13. The father wasn't content with our one-woman system of marriage; his wife finally had enough and they divorced. Finances were difficult for this single-parent, small-farm family when the dad went his own way. He didn't help out with child support or alimony. After years of farm and factory work, the mother went into real estate sales, through which she began to enjoy a reasonable degree of financial security. However, after about five years, she sold everything she owned, mortgaged to the maximum and bought a run-down lake shore resort, consisting of 12 cabins and a six-unit motel.

The whole family worked hard to update and remodel the buildings. However, the grown son began to have difficulty finding an outside job. He worked periodically on repair jobs here and there, picking up valuable skills but repeatedly returned home broke and discouraged.

This energetic mother finally was realizing success with her life and had raised her goals. She decided to become a millionaire. How could she accomplish this and help her son at the same time? One day, an idea came to her: With her real estate expertise and his handyman skills, together they sought out run-down properties, fixed them up and resold them for profit. Now they both have a better vision of what the future holds.

Another mom was getting discouraged because her 24-year-old son was chronically unemployed. He tried and tried to find a job, but was not successful and had become very discouraged. Saying he couldn't stand any more rejection, he quit trying and began hanging out at the corner bar, sleeping late and watching too much TV.

Frantic to help her son, Mom sent his name to all the armed services. Very shortly, the phone started ringing and soon the young man was signed up in the Marines. He's being trained in computers. Upon discharge he'll have a skill which, it is hoped, will translate into employment.

One daughter, having graduated from college six months previously, still was unemployed. She'd become very depressed and even quit caring. She spent most of her day sleeping or watching TV. Finally, Dad decided to get involved.

In desperation he set up informational contacts and a few job interviews with business associates. He made sure his daughter kept the appointments. After each interview, Dad would call his friend to see how his daughter had done. When she finally did get a job, she realized she had to give her dad some of the credit. Now it was up to her to perform well and live up to his expectations.

In general, the state of transition or growth that many nesters are in tends to make them fearful, anxious and ill-tempered. They are apt to take their frustrations out on the people closest to them, the ones they love the most. Home is where they can relax, be themselves and still be loved and accepted for who they are—warts and all. At this time, communications are extremely important, but are often difficult to maintain. If the pressures of school or job become too great, some young adults take subconscious refuge in anxiety, illness and depression, and a few even become suicidal. Concern from a loving family will often turn the tide for them.

Social life. Some nesters come under severe pressure in their social life. Either they are overly busy or there is nothing to do. There are problems in either case. If their social life is too busy, their time is taken up with dates, dances and parties. Then family responsibilities, household chores and family communications suffer. If their social life is nil, then the nester can go into a depression and use the family home as an escape— rather than seeking out old friends or making new ones. How is a nester to find the right balance? A word from parents can alert a nester to the fact that he or she is getting too busy or that he or she is stagnating. Then, appropriate action should be taken. If it's a busy time, the nester should cut back, schedule time better and become reacquainted with the family. If it's a lonely time, the nester should make an effort to get involved in outside activities.

Susie, an unmarried nester, was suffering with a case of the blues following the marriage of her two best friends. The blues turned into a mild form of depression, which went on for months. Her mom suggested that she develop a hobby or find a new interest. "No, there's nothing that I'm interested in right now," she glumly replied. Mom wouldn't give up, though. Remembering that Susie liked to play bridge, her mother suggested that she check out the local bridge center. The daughter replied, "You need a partner to do that." Mom persisted and offered to be that partner until her daughter found someone else. Susie swiftly found a partner in another young woman she met there. But better yet, one year later, that bridge center is where she met her future husband and father of her son.

An example of being too busy is 20-year-old Shelley, who had just made up with her steady boyfriend, Tom, after a quarrel. Night after night, Shelley waved goodnight to the family as she and Tom spent every free minute together. Shelley's responsibilities at home were neglected, leading to problems with her parents. Three days in a row she brushed aside mom's ever-increasing requests to, "Please do something with your room today, Shelley. You know Grandma is coming to visit this weekend." But Shelley only answered, "Sure, later," as she ran out the door.

Then, there's Mike. He is stagnating. Several of his friends recently left for college, and another buddy is going steady with a special girl. So Mike finds himself suddenly without friends. He stays home night after night, watching television and snacking. He's gaining weight at an alarming rate. Realizing that Mike needs a new interest, Dad can suggest he join a bowling team or take dance lessons.

Many nesters are experiencing stress regarding school, job and social life. An awareness of these pressures is a first step in relieving them. Support from parents can go a long way in helping to relieve these situations. If pressures can't be relieved, then just sharing them with a caring family member will often help the situation.

Pressures that parents endure

Having an adult offspring in the house can put a strain on the parents. What's a parent to do about household chores, use of the car, going to church, etc., if there is disagreement as to who is to do what and when? In this section, we will look at various topics that have caused pressures on parents which, in turn, inhibit communication.

In our survey, topics mentioned that created differences between parents and nesters were:

Transportation
Religious activities
Recreation
Household chores
Job-hunting

Sex
Rearing of a grandchild
Carelessness with clothes
Friends
Lack of job or schooling
Sleeping late
Kitchen use after hours and failure to clean up
Lack of personal cleanliness
Uncommunicativeness
Disagreements about politics, investments and trends
Jealousy
Despondency
Rock music
Alcohol and drugs
Choice of vocabulary
Consideration of family members
Friends invading the home too often
Treatment of siblings
Dirty dishes left around house
Unpaid long-distance phone bills
Refusal to take care of mail
Borrowing money
Smoking in the home

An especially distasteful situation occurred in one home. The son went to a major city to work and for a while all went well. Then he lost his job and had to move into a rundown hotel. Finally, he phoned his mom and asked if he could come home to regroup. After an affirmative reply, he came home—"but brought his friends with him," Mom related. "His friends?" "Yes," she replied, *"cockroaches!"*

Mom called the pest control people and had them fumigate the house. Perhaps, if one suspects that an returning offspring's belongings might harbor pests, it might be wise to launder or dry clean all incoming clothes and empty all boxes outside.

Since many of these topics are interrelated, they are dealt with generally in the following section, called *"The Bill of Rights."* Some irritants are treated individually since they seem to be common concerns for many families.

Unsolicited advice from nesters on how to raise younger siblings. The following incident shows how two nesters felt they had spotted a problem and told their mother how to solve it. "One Sunday," writes a mother of eight children, "Two of the older girls, Mary and Kathy, had come to me separately to say how upset they were about Sam, their 15-year-old brother. He had gotten a job and bought a moped. Mary felt that Sam had gotten "pretty egotistical now that he had his own money." Kathy said that because Sam was now the oldest son at home (two older brothers had recently moved out), he thought this gave him the rights and freedoms that his older brothers had when they lived at home. She complained that he wasn't helping around the house anymore and that he was staying out late at night—much too late for a 15-year-old! She suggested he should do his fair share of work at home and come in earlier at night. In other words, the older sisters felt their mother should lay out some rules for Sam.

"When Mary complained about Sam, I just shrugged it off," wrote the mother. "But later, when Kathy did the same, I told everyone, 'It looks like we have to have a family conference—and it'll be tonight!' Later, around the dining room table, Mary and Kathy aired their complaints about Sam for 15 long minutes. 'Okay, you two,' replied Sam, 'is it my turn now?' Then he gave his side of the story. His job took many of his formerly free hours, so some of Kathy's charges were true—he wasn't helping around the house as much as before. But Mary and Kathy had to realize that they worked only 40 hours a week, while he attended school full-time and in addition was working 15 hours a week as a busboy. Some nights he had to work till closing at 1 a.m., so that's why he was out late. It followed then that he slept late on weekends and missed out on some of the Saturday morning household chores. 'Sure I've got more money now,' continued Sam, 'but I worked hard for it, so I think that I can spend it on some things that I need and want—like my moped that I use to get to work.'

"There was some arguing back and forth," the mother wrote.

"At one point Kathy wanted to go to her room, but dad wouldn't let her. I was getting discouraged over the bickering. But dad just sat back and listened. Finally, an hour later, the air had cleared and they were all talked out. Resentments dissolved because nothing was left to brew inside the girls."

With open communication, it was possible to resolve the festering resentments the older sisters were feeling and had expressed. Family discussions are not always easy nor pleasant, but are necessary in restoring good feelings between young and older siblings.

Checking in. Neglecting to inform the people with whom you live about your timetable can cause concern and worry. It is only common consideration for nesters to inform their family if they are not planning on eating or sleeping at home some night. Checking in makes for a smooth-running home.

Checking in about a change in sleeping arrangements is more serious than missing meals. When a nester doesn't come home as expected, this can cause real worry for the parents.

Here's what happened when a nester didn't inform her parents in advance of her overnight plans: Ellen had been to a party with her boyfriend, and during the course of the evening, she and a girlfriend made plans for early the next morning. To them, it made sense for Ellen to sleep over at her girlfriend's house. So, at midnight, Ellen's boyfriend went home and Ellen and her girlfriend went on to Ellen's home to get some clothes for the next day. Then, so her parents wouldn't worry, she made a large note—two feet by three feet—telling her parents of her plans. This she taped to her bedroom door. Ellen's mother woke up at around 3 a.m. and realized that she hadn't heard Ellen come in to say that she was home. She got up to check Ellen's bedroom. In the darkness she walked right past the oversized note and on into the empty bedroom. Panicking, she woke her husband and they called Ellen's boyfriend's parents, who said that their son had come home hours ago. They didn't know where Ellen was.

Ellen's parents worried and prayed for several hours. Finally at 6 a.m., they called the police. Walking down the hallway to answer the policeman's knock, they passed their daughter's bedroom and in the early dawn light they saw her note. All those agonizing hours need not have happened if Ellen had awakened her mother when she stopped at home at midnight or, better yet, had made her plans in advance and told her parents ahead of time. When families live together, it's only considerate to leave notes when leaving an empty house. Inform the next arrival when he or she can expect other family members to come home. A postscript on the note saying there is something special in the house to eat is usually a warm fuzzy.

Transportation. Cars, bikes and buses (transportation in general) are often an area of disagreement between nesters and their parents. Should the nester get his or her own car? If so, what kind of model, make and year? How will it be paid for? Will the parent need to co-sign a loan? What about insurance and repairs? If the nester has his or her own car, there is generally no problem, unless the nester runs short of gas money or can't make monthly car payments. However, it's a different story if the nester needs to use a family vehicle. How does the family go about sharing a car, gas expenses, and shopping chores? It may be helpful to see how other families handle this problem.

It's best if plans are made in advance, so that optimal use is made of the car. If a nester needs to use the car to go to work, and if mother needs to have a package delivered near the nester's place of work, it seems only reasonable that the nester deliver the package. But it is not reasonable if Mom waits till the last moment to tell the nester while he or she goes out the door. Dropping off the package may make him or her late for work. The key to sharing a car is planning and stating needs ahead of time, so that no one need be greatly inconvenienced.

When a nester uses a family car, several arrangements can be made to share gas expenses. Some parents charge their nester a flat fee per mile when he or she uses the family car. Other parents ask only that their nester replenish the gas used. A few parents hand their offspring the family gasoline credit card, intending that it be used sparingly and that the nester pay his or her share of the bill.

Household chores. "A thousand and one excuses the kids have got—math or baseball—not to do their jobs," says Vicky, a mother of 15 children. Getting cooperation from family members for household chores is often a difficult task, especially from nesters. It seems like there are never enough hands to do the jobs that need to be done. With some planning, this problem can be lessened.

Being very specific about who does what, and when they do it, seems to work best for most families. Work sheets listing various jobs can be posted in a prominent place. The refrigerator door is a good place to post this list, since everyone seems to check in there fairly often. One family's list reads like this:

Joan: *wash breakfast dishes*
Liz: *sweep back stairs and basement*
Nathan: *collect and bring dirty clothes to the basement*
Martina: *sort and fold clothes*
Stefan: *wash supper dishes and clean dining room*
John: *make beds, vacuum living room and stairs.*[10]

One mother is retaining responsibility for her household by saying, "It's my duty as the parent to supervise my children. They live in this house and are responsible for some upkeep. It requires an effort, but I think each family can devise its own method."[11]

However, there are some nesters who rarely help around the home unless asked specifically to do so. One nester even replied, "I shouldn't have to help around the house because, after all, I pay rent."

Fortunately, most nesters do help with household chores. As a nudge, nesters can be reminded that if they had their own apartment, they'd have to pay rent and do the household chores as well, unless they had enough money to hire a cleaning service. Nesters have been known to help in the following ways:

cleaning	*house & plant sitting*	*care of pets*
laundry	*lawn care*	*garage upkeep*
cooking	*house repair*	*car care*
painting	*garbage removal*	*shopping*

In delegating responsibility for chores around the home, it's important to be fair. A busy nester is not going to have as much free time to work around the home as the sibling who has the summer off and time on his or her hands. This is why it's so important to set up a schedule of duties together that will fit in with you and your nester's lifestyle.

If you do set up such a schedule, perhaps one day your nester will cooperate with household chores as the following nester does. He writes, "I do anything I can to help my mom—she's overworked!"

Religious activities. The church gives the family a code of morals and invests it with a touch of holiness that helps keep it stable. "The family that prays together stays together."[12]

Convictions about God and church vary from family to family. It cannot be denied, though, that belief in God and religion play an integral part in many families. One mother tells how she views God. "I have a personal intimacy with God. I don't believe He's a blob in the sky bye 'n bye. It's like a marriage. One day you love Him, and the next day you have a fight with Him. What happens in the kitchen shakes the heavens. I tell my kids, I believe that what happens in this life affects eternity! Perhaps Maria, my daughter, says it even more clearly, 'We've got a God in our house and we use Him.'"[13]

When nesters and their families agree on religious beliefs and practices, then the nesting time can be very satisfying spiritually. This was true for about half of the families contacted in the survey mentioned in the preface. But, of course, not all families agree on religious activities. When this occurs, it is important to communicate preferences and then discuss how to deal with them. Religious conviction and belief in a living, active God is a step which no one can force upon another person. Each person must be free to choose. If a grown offspring is forced to accompany the family to church, there isn't much spiritual value for either the nester or his family. God gave man a free will, and grown children, as well as everyone else, must be free to make their own decision in this regard. If parents are concerned about the example being given to younger siblings by a nester not attending church, then a family discussion may be in order. If, as a parent of a nester, you feel that God is important, then perhaps by your actions and loving acceptance—not condemnation—you will have an influence on those with whom you live.

House rules. House rules are a big problem for some nesting families. Who does have the final say, parents or nester? From the consensus of respondents to the survey, it does seem that the parents should have the final say. As one daughter says, "I don't try and change my mom's ideas anymore. After all, this is her territory."

A father writes, "Young people grow up in a home and they come to feel that it is theirs. In a sense it is theirs, but unless you as a parent take authority over the actions of the residents, there will be no order. If there is no order, chaos can result. Be gentle, but firm." He continues, "There should be guidelines for young adults to follow, such as:

- *You can eat after meals, if you clean up the kitchen.*

- *You can have friends over and, within reason, they can help themselves to the food in the house.*

- *You can have your own bedroom or share one with a brother or sister, but you have to take responsibility to keep it clean and neat.*

- *You have your rights as one of our children, but your rights are not to infringe upon the rights of other family members."*

Professional advisors also agree that it's best if there are firm guidelines. "Neubauer, a marriage therapist in New York, is firm about insisting that if such an arrangement (nesting) becomes necessary, the group should work out every detail in advance—chores, finances and even at what point an amicable separation needs to take place. 'Otherwise, just deciding who is supposed to take out the garbage can become a major disaster,' she said. 'Everyone must know exactly what is expected of the others.'"[14]

One mother comes right to the point. "This is a family. This is not a hotel where you come and go. Even if you're an adult, you have to abide by the rules. If you guys think you're going to eat and sleep here and spend all your money on stereos and cars, you have another cookie coming. Because, then I feel I'm being used by my kids. I'm a very compassionate woman, but I'm not a sucker."[15]

Parents' Bill of Rights

(Written by a father of several nesters)

1. *Expect help from nesters with household and yard chores in the amount of 1/2 hour per day plus 2 hours on Saturday or their day off.*

2. *Expect contributions according to nesters' means toward their room and board.*

3. *Expect nesters to keep their area (bedroom) of the house clean daily.*

4. *Expect nesters to abide by the rules of the home regarding smoking and drinking and inform their visiting friends of these rules also.*

5. *Expect nesters to be communicative and respectful toward other family members.*

6. *Expect nesters to be participating members of the family—meals, recreation, etc.*

Nesters' Bill of Rights

(Written by a 22-year-old nester)

1. *Deserves respect from parents as an adult.*

2. *Deserves respect from parents regarding the decisions nesters make—*
that these are decisions made by an adult, rather than decisions made by a minor.

3. *Parents must be willing to give a nester the needed independence to grow as an*
adult, i.e. don't smother nester and prevent him or her from developing to his or
her full potential.

Siblings' Bill of Rights

(Written by three younger siblings of a nester)

1. *The big kid shouldn't tell his or her brothers and sisters what to do or tell the*
parents how to raise the other kids.

2. *The grown-up kids living at home should respect the privacy of the younger kids.*

3. *The grown-up kids should get the same treatment as the other kids—no special*
favors for them because they are grown-up.

Openness in relating

Communications under the pressures of nesting can be difficult. Sometimes, these difficulties erupt into anger. Using body language can help families raise awareness. Listening, negotiation, and compromise help nesting families. During communication, parents discover pressures that nesters endure, and nesters realize pressures that parents sustain. When families construct and honor guidelines, such as a Bill of Rights, communications flow and nesting can be a happy family time.

CHAPTER SEVEN

Money matters
—it really does

"The rural family in Ireland lives, on the average, on a farm too small to be subdivided any further, and therefore only one son can inherit the land. The father can pick any one of them he likes, but he does not indicate his choice until he is good and ready. The result is that the sons who do not emigrate or drift off to jobs in the cities stay home and go on working, in a position of total subordination to the old man. And if they should get a side job like road mending, their wages are supposed to go into their father's pocket, and he is quite capable of turning up himself on payday to collect whatever money they may have earned."[1]

Finances are a major reason for nesters to stay home or to return home. The most highly volatile money issues are room and board, tuition, checking accounts, budgets, loans, health insurance and taxes. We really need a lot of love and communication to get through this money maze!

Recession and inflation

Yesterday, today, and probably tomorrow, the majority of nesters come home, or stay home, on a temporary or a permanent basis, because of money matters. Today, the cyclical financial problems of inflation and recession are especially burdensome for our young people. This may be their first exposure to the fact that the value of a dollar has been decreasing year after year. They're learning economic truths the hard way. Because of inflation, we spend more money, but it buys less. With recession, there are more people looking for work than jobs available.

A growing number of young people are discovering that independence is simply beyond their means. "My salary just doesn't keep up with inflation. I don't want to live in some rundown apartment building," writes one young woman. "So I live with my folks, even though it's not what I prefer."

Many young adults have grown up with a high standard of living. They are used to affluence, reports psychiatrist Paul Kingsley. To leave their parents' home and support themselves fully means they'd have to live on a lower standard. They're not as willing to do that as earlier generations were.[2] But many nesters just can't afford both high apartment rent and monthly car payments. Another economic lesson they're quickly learning is that in a recession, businesses are forced to lay off employees because of cutbacks in production.

Some nesters are unemployed and forced to rely on their parents for room and board. Because they're young, they are the victims of "last hired, first fired." Some students and low-salaried working nesters also need support from their parents. This comes as a shock to some parents, who never thought that their grown child might need help with everyday living expenses. But times have changed since today's parents of nesters were in their 20s.

Legally, our financial obligations to our children ends when they reach 18. We've fed and clothed them, we've paid for eyeglasses, orthodontists, schooling and in some cases, car and college expenses. On top of this, we've loved them with all our hearts. "Isn't that enough?" some parents ask. "Just how far do we have to carry this grown child? We've started thinking of retirement and travel plans and along comes our adult offspring who needs money. Are we supposed to sacrifice our retirement dreams, our dreams of freedom, so we can bail him out?"

But who can say "no" to nesters who need a place to hang their hats because they are so perilously low on funds? How can we refuse them car loans or help with their college expenses if they need it and we have the means? How can we say "no" without feeling guilty? And if we do say "yes," can we really say it without a trace of resentment?

Studies show that money is high on the list of causes of trouble in a family. We hear and talk about the breakdown of communications, drug and alcohol problems and behavior problems with our children. However, unspoken money problems are the most volatile issues to trigger hot tempers within a family. And they are often set up by ignorance and insensitivity. One nester indicated on the survey that he had "no idea" of the amount of his parents' combined annual income or their monthly mortgage payment. How can he be expected to be sympathetic to their financial problems if he isn't aware of their financial obligations along with their income?

A spirit of ungratefulness

Three fathers personally conveyed their feelings of resentment toward their nesters. Not only aren't the young adults contributing room and board, but one dad is footing all college expenses. The fathers felt their offspring were ungrateful. One father, Ed, stated, "Not asking for room and board was the biggest single mistake I have made with my five grown children, who freely move in and out." He feels that not asking for room and board gave his children the idea that he has lots of money. So now, not only do they not pay room and board, but they also ask him for extra money when they run short of cash. If he had been more open with his children about how much money he made, and about his fixed monthly expenses, he feels this problem would have been avoided.

The second father is a classic example of a parent who sacrificed his personal wants to save money for his children's expenses. For one son, he footed the bills through an undergraduate degree, a master's degree, and a doctorate. He also frequently sent $100 for extra expenses, when his son asked for it. Yet, after all this financial help, the son didn't acknowledge his indebtedness. One day his son came home and, during a conversation with his dad, claimed that he never received any financial help from his father!

Perhaps the argument was based on a misunderstanding. However, this denial of his help, and the underlying ingratitude, have made Dad bitter toward his son. He now suggests that a parent save all receipts and canceled checks so he can prove his financial assistance, if necessary.

A third resentful father feels that his children take him, and his money, for granted. "It's as if they feel they have a God-given right to my support," he says. He believes that there is nothing in his paternal contract that says he has to give money to adult children, especially when they don't even say "thank you."

The best way to ease these growing tensions is through communication. By talking about their feelings and opinions, families can smooth the tension and ease resentment. It may turn out that our children are simply so unsophisticated and ignorant about money matters that we aren't looking at the issue of money through the same eyes. Or perhaps, since parental financial resources were something they could count on when they were 8, 10 and 12, they assume nothing will change when they are 18, 25 and 30.

Perhaps we should start with the financial education of our children. If you haven't communicated honestly in the past about this subject, now is a beautiful time to begin! Start by talking about money in general. It'll be the first step toward making life with your nesters free from under-the-surface financial tensions. Build up to talking about those hidden resentments and unresolved money problems. Bring it all out into the light. Let them know where the money comes from and where it goes, month by month. Discuss the financial goals and objectives of both parents and nesters. Talk about budgeting, loan agreements, grocery and utility bills, school expenses, checking accounts, health insurance, taxes, and most of all, the specific financial sacrifices of the parents for their children without seeming to throw it in their faces.

If we are open and honest about family resources as our children grow, we can avoid a lot of ungratefulness and resentment about money while our children are in the nester stage. If, after our children have reached adulthood, they still seem to be unaware of our true financial situation, correct the misimpressions and they won't expect unrealistic financial aid.

Room and board

The No. 1 controversial financial issue between a nester and his or her parents is room and board. Some parents feel guilty for wanting their nester to help with room and board. After all, we don't want to squeeze blood out of a turnip, especially if it's our own turnip! Yet, we don't want to be used financially, be unappreciated for all the things we've given our children or see our children grow up unaware of the value of a dollar. Imagine being the parent who heard "through the grapevine" that her nester son was bragging to his friends about the "free ride" he was getting by living at home. As tempers flew, so did the nester with all his belongings—right out the door!

In my survey, only about two-thirds of the nesters who are working full-time pay room and board. The average amount paid is $125 a month, with a range of $75 to $300 a month. This means that about one-third of the nesters who are working full-time pay no room and board. Hardly any of the nesters who are students, either full- or part-time, pay room and board. If parents don't need the money, they can secretly save it and give it back to the nester as he or she moves out. This can then be used as a nest egg to help the nester get his or her feet on the ground.

To pay or not to pay—that is the question

All this leads to the question: should nesters pay room and board? If they have a good job, and if their parents don't feel they can absorb the extra costs the nesters' presence creates, it becomes an easy question to answer: obviously, yes. But if the nesters have poor-paying jobs, and the parents are fairly well established, the answer is no longer so clear cut. There were various reasons why some nesters do not pay room and board:

"Dad won't take it," wrote one young man.
"He usually doesn't have enough money," replied a mother.
"Never discussed," responded another mother.
"She's not paying anything. She was never asked to contribute," one parent replied.

In the following example, son and mother gave their opinions on a nester's payment of room and board. The nester is 26 years old, attending school part-time and working part-time, with an annual income of $12,000. He felt that paying room and board was unnecessary. But his mother wrote, "He feels we don't need the money and he does." (This family was in an upper income bracket.) Often the problem is a lack of communication.

The following example indicates the beneficial results of talking about this problem. Sandi, who is working full-time and is concerned about helping out financially in the family home, has never been asked for room and board. Yet she doesn't want to be financially dependent on her family. She also wants to continue to live at home. Her parents have never talked about money with Sandi, and she knew that they would be very reluctant to accept any room and board payments. So, she decided she would speak with her mother, and carefully bring up the subject.

She began by asking about the household expenses. Because Sandi was showing an interest in the family finances, the conversation gradually got around to the subject of room and board. Sandi explained that she didn't want to be financially dependent on her folks, that she wanted to be treated as a responsible adult. Her mother came to understand and accept this fact, and soon her father did also.

Today, Sandi is paying room and board, equal to what it would cost her to live in a nearby apartment (including rent, utilities, food and laundry expenses). Her parents view Sandi with more respect now, and Sandi is satisfied that, even though she chooses to live in her parents' home, she is paying her own way.

Here's another example of a satisfactory solution to the room and board problem. When the Browns decided to ask their daughter, Paula, for room and board, she was agreeable to the suggestion. Paula had been feeling a trifle guilty that she had not been paying her folks, so when they brought up the subject, Paula felt relieved because she hadn't known how to bring up the matter herself. She knew that her take-home pay was very little, but she would be getting two substantial raises within the next year. So, rather than setting a flat room and board fee now, and having to readjust it later when Paula's income increased, they all agreed to 15 percent of Paula's take-home pay as her room and board payment. In this family, talking about the situation eased the tensions and solved the problem for everyone.

Unfortunately, not all offspring are as willing as Paula and Sandi to contribute their fair share. If you are getting the feeling that your son or daughter might not be as agreeable to contribute as the two nesters above, read on. The following family story portrays a nester reluctant to contribute toward his keep. His response even bordered on belligerence.

The Smiths' 22-year-old son, Ben, was a rerooster who had returned home after college graduation. He has been back in the family nest for over a year, and has been steadily employed all that time. Even though his job is at an entry-level position with the customary low pay, Mr. and Mrs. Smith talked over the matter privately and decided that Ben should start contributing toward room and board. One day Mrs. Smith broke the news to Ben. She was met by a frozen stare. Ben asked belligerently, "How much do ya want?" "Well," Mom replied, "I think it's something that we should talk about. Dad and I aren't exactly sure how much." Ben was unwilling to discuss the matter. "When you decide, let me know," he snarled and stomped out of the house. Several days later, after serving Ben's favorite supper, Mrs. Smith tried to talk to him again. She told him that she and dad were serious about room and board, and had Ben given it any further thought? His reply was, "Ya, I suppose I havta if you guys say so. How much do ya want?"

Now Ben was reluctantly agreeable, but an amount remained to be determined. "Let's look at how much take-home pay you get each month, Ben," Mom replied. "We don't want it to be hardship on you, but we do feel that you should be paying something." Mrs. Smith picked up a pencil and paper and wrote down Ben's monthly take-home pay, which was $1,000. Then she asked him to write down his fixed monthly expenses, which totaled $400, leaving him $600 on which to live. Ben was surprised it was so much. He had no idea where it all went! Mom suggested Ben pay $25 a week for room and board (she had discussed it privately with her husband and this is what they had agreed upon, if it was acceptable to their son). Ben's payment to his parents would total $100 a month, and in the light of the extra $600 Ben now realized he had, $100 didn't look out of line. It would still leave him with $500 each month to do with as he pleased. At the same time, he would have a feeling of paying his own way.

The Smiths' communicated effectively by confronting their nester with the issue. If lack of room and board payment is a problem in your family that you have not been able to deal with, consider the reasons why you may want to ask. Do you need the money to help meet the bills? If the answer is yes, the request is not based on greed, it is a necessity. If you don't need the extra money, consider the following:

Reason for paying when not needed by parents

Perhaps parents are not doing their nesters a favor by sparing them the financial responsibility of paying room and board, if they have an income or could be earning an income. Are parents preparing nesters to live outside the home in the real world of high prices? By not paying, we allow our nesters to escalate to a higher standard of living than they may be able to maintain later when they are on their own. Probably, they do not even think about budgeting for rent and food. Consequently, you may be forcing your nester to stay on in your home longer than may be good for all concerned. For all these reasons, nesters with low-paying or even part-time jobs may especially need the responsibility of paying room and board—ironic as it seems—if for no other reason than to prepare them for the high costs of paying for their own basic needs when they do move out.

It seems to be, and reasonably so, that the less income the parents make, the more often (and in larger amounts) the nester pays room and board. For example, one survey family's annual income was $20,000, and their nester paid $150 monthly. Another family, whose annual income was in the $150,000 range, did not require a room and board payment. The parents didn't need the additional income, so it was difficult for them to justify asking for room and board. Thus, it seems easier for low and middle income parents to educate their children in financial independence.

Types of room and board

The following four cases illustrate how some families deal with room and board issues:

• The Johnsons have two nesting daughters, in addition to eight other children. These two daughters pay the electric bill between themselves, which usually amounts to about $30 a week for each.

• One male nester, 26 years old, is laid off. But when he is working he pays room and board every other week, on payday, $150 per paycheck.

• Two brothers, age 22 and 25, both working full-time, "pay $15 to $20 a week depending on wages and whether lunches are packed and dinner eaten at home regularly."

• A fourth nester is a 38-year-old male with no siblings. He pays all household bills except mortgage payments, house insurance and phone. This means that he pays the electric bills, home repair bills and taxes. In addition, he pays room and board of $80 to $125 a month. He is more established in his job and can contribute more than younger nesters.

Sweat equity. However, some parents don't feel they can ask for room and board when their nester is going to college, even if he or she has a part-time job. It's usually true that nesters who are students have little or no extra money for room and board; that's why many of them are living at home.

To ensure a feeling of worth, appreciation and respect, however, how about another contribution—in the form of assigned household chores? Here are some examples: Dale is a 19-year-old, full-time student with a part-time job. He has agreed to scrub and wax the kitchen floor, wash the car and mow the lawn each week in exchange for room and board, in addition to straightening his room and helping with the dinner dishes every evening. Tammy and Joan, 19 and 20, are both working part-time and attending school part-time. They "don't pay room and board directly," writes their mother, "but they do extra work for us around the house, such as laundry, heavy duty cleaning and shopping."

Still other nesters are paying off school debts. For example, Jim, a college graduate, worked part-time while going to school and still was forced to take out a loan to cover his tuition. After graduation, Jim didn't like the loan hanging over his head and wanted to get it paid off as quickly as possible. He discussed this with his parents and they agreed that he could live at home, rent-free, as long as he paid $400 a month on his college loan. Since his degree enabled him to secure a good job, he was able to make this large monthly payment. With his parents' help of a rent-free room, he was able to reduce his loan balance by a substantial amount each month.

One mother had a novel response to my questionnaire: "Listening to me is part of the rent they pay!"

Many nesters are living in their parents' homes because of their desire of upward mobility—they frankly intend eventually to live better than their parents. So, they are living cheaply at home in order to build a nest egg. Phil Donahue described it thus: "Remember the traditional Norman Rockwell view of America? The parents got off of the boat at Ellis Island and made their way up the street. The father worked hard and he and his wife sent their children out into the world to do better than they did. Well, most of the people in our generation did better than our parents. Not because we were smarter, but because we had a society that seemed to absorb us and give us more opportunities than our folks had, and in many cases there was less prejudice. Our parents wanted us to do better than they did and we want our kids to do better than we did."[3]

But now this attitude often means that young adults will rely on their parents for a prolonged amount of time. Now, it takes more time to build the bigger nest eggs that satisfy the growing appetites of young people.

Some nesters are saving money for big-ticket items, such as a down payment on a home. Lea's family handled the situation like this: her marriage to Tom had broken up, leaving Lea feeling rejected, despondent and nearly penniless. In addition, her 2-year-old son, Scott, was an added financial responsibility, though he was also a ray of sunshine for Lea. The young mother wanted to save money for a down payment on a little two-bedroom house that she visualized for herself and Scott. Her parents were glad to help them out with temporary, free housing while Lea was in this state of transition. They not only helped their daughter financially, but emotionally as well, with this embracing gesture. They felt that had they insisted on rent, this would only have delayed the day when Lea could realize her dream of a home for herself and her child.

Summertime College Nesters. Some nesters are periodic live-ins. College students fall into this category. They come home for Christmas break, interim break, and summer vacation. Most of them work during the summer and save their checks to pay for next year's tuition. Few families expect this category of nester to pay room and board. But other arrangements can be worked out, such as a sharing of household chores. Help with family chores is really necessary when a family has several college-age students who often arrive with a bang— hungry, loaded with dirty laundry, extra clothes and furniture. To complete the picture, they also bring with them an increase in the noise level in the house: loud voices, blaring stereo, and a phone ringing off the hook! (How do their friends seem to know the very hour of their arrival?) It's an exciting time of reunion, sharing events of months past, and seeing a new maturity in the students. But it's still a shock having them home again. With young people away at college, parents get used to a certain quietness, and a gentle, prevailing peace. Then, suddenly, it's bedlam! A happy bedlam, but confusion nevertheless. Dad can't find his shorts, socks, newspaper, milk or car. Yet he is forever tripping over clothes, friends and shoes!

Along with all this turmoil comes extra work, such as additional grocery shopping, cooking, laundry and cleaning. It seems only right that these periodic nesters assume some share of the extra household chores. The Olson family currently have three college-age scholars who came home each spring. After the initial greetings and exchanges of news and feelings, they divide the summer chores. Last summer, Mary offered to keep the two cars clean and do the grocery shopping. Pete volunteered for the yard work. Ginger kept the washing machine loaded and the clean clothes neatly folded into proper piles. With this happy arrangement and relatively easy workload, there was plenty of time to enjoy each other's company for the next few months, without squabbles. Mom and Dad knew, too, that it would be as quiet as a morgue again come September. In one way, they miss all the frenzied summer activities, but just as soon as they'd begin to enjoy the quiet, it would be time for Christmas to roll around and the students would be back....

Families who don't talk about room and board may suffer the fate of the Nelson family. Here were traditional parents willing to help out, but who, through lack of communication about finances, were pushed to the limit and reacted in the extreme.

A real estate agent related the following tale: Mr. and Mrs. Nelson said that they wanted to put their home up for sale and buy a smaller one with only one bedroom. They had a medium-priced home with four bedrooms. Their children were all grown, but they had the tendency to keep moving back in, without paying their way.

The first time the married daughter returned, she had one baby and was separated from her husband. The next time she returned, she was divorced and had two youngsters. The Nelsons' son also freely moved in and out of their home between jobs. The parents didn't know how to tell their grown children that they really didn't feel it was right for them to move in without paying room and board. The only thing they could think of was to move into a one-bedroom home, and subtly tell their children there was no room in the inn. They subsequently sold their home and bought an elegant, one-bedroom condo. Now the grown children and grandchildren come to visit, but they can't stay since there are no extra bedrooms.

Looking at this move as an objective observer, you might think that the Nelsons over-reacted a little, and that a simple heart-to-heart talk with their children could have saved their large home. Yet, they're happy with their choice and their new home.

Following is an example in direct contrast to the Nelsons, who felt that they should have been getting room and board, but didn't know how to ask for it. Mr. and Mrs. Erickson didn't want room and board, and said so. But Ron, a nester who is a college graduate working full-time as an engineer, wanted to contribute. Mrs. Erickson refused his offer, reasoning that she and Dad didn't have a need for the extra money, and were just glad to have their son back home after college. It sounds almost too good to be true for Ron, but let's take a closer look.

Some parents want so intensely for their adult children to live with them that they won't allow them to pay room and board.

They say they merely want to do something for their children, and that they have plenty of room. They also may say they do not need the money. But could there be more to it than that?

Could it be that these parents don't want to accept room and board because they want—perhaps subconsciously—to keep their relationship on the parent-child plateau? With this arrangement, the parents are seemingly still in control; they can continue to tell their children what to do. By accepting room and board, they would have to treat the nester as an adult. And that's something to think about! One mother who refuses rent from her daughter, a 24-year-old sales rep, states, "I am determined that things in this house should remain the way my husband and I want them."[4]

There is another option. In lieu of pocketing room and board when it is not needed by the parents, families could decide to give the funds to a homeless shelter. Or, as mentioned previously, quietly save the money as a going-away gift when the adult child finally does move out.

For a peek at rent variations across America, read further to learn which cities have the most expensive rates and which cities the least.[5]

10 Most-Expensive Cities		10 Least-Expensive Cities	
Location	Monthly Rental	Location	Monthly Rental
Honolulu, HI	$980	Oklahoma City, OK	$305
New York, NY	775	Colorado Springs, CO	325
Boston, MA	765	Austin, TX	330
San Jose, CA	735	Wichita, KS	330
Washington, DC	725	San Antonio, TX	330
San Francisco, CA	715	Tulsa, OK	335
Ventura, CA	680	Houston, TX	350
Los Angeles, CA	675	Pensacola, FL	355
Chicago, IL	650	Tucson, AZ	365
Hartford, CT	620	Salt Lake City, UT	365

Knowing the average rent charged in their area will give families a guide in deciding on a room and board figure.

Checking accounts

Often, adolescents' first glimpse of the banking industry is a savings account. Then, when they have to start paying bills, it's time to open a checking account. Later, when they need a loan, it is only natural that they approach their own bank first to ask for financial assistance.

Even though they have no prior credit rating, they have a definite advantage if the bank records indicate that they have handled a checking account without incurring overdrafts or bouncing checks. Since proper handling of a checking account indicates fiscal responsibility, and since banks feel an obligation to accommodate the legitimate credit needs of their depositors, responsible nesters should get the loans they seek. It is a necessity when considering future bank transactions that nesters remain friendly with their bankers.

Most people use checking accounts to pay bills by mail and to pay for purchases. It is certainly easier and safer than carrying cash around. Unfortunately, however, many young people have trouble making sure that they don't overdraw the account. Erma Bombeck humorously related that one of her children wrote the bank a check to cover an overdraft!

In addition, many young people have trouble keeping track of canceled checks. One nester, Roy, is a good example: Roy regularly asked his mother to get him money orders for his car payment, insurance and charge card bills. Finally, she suggested that Roy open a checking account for paying his bills, which he did. Months went by, and one day his mom asked Roy how his checking account was working out. "Oh, I'm not sure," he answered. "I just write checks and then the bank sends them back to me. I've got them saved in my dresser drawer. What am I supposed to do with them now?"

Mom told Roy that he should check his bank statement to see that neither he, nor the bank, had made any errors. Later that week, Roy spread his checking account statements all over the dining room table and worked for several baffling hours comparing the canceled checks with his own records and the bank's statements. He finally gave up in defeat. But a good night's sleep gave him new energy, and he tackled the pile of papers again the following evening. At length, he told his mom that he was off only a couple of dollars and that he wasn't "gonna worry about that little bit!" Despite his imprecise approach to his checking balance, Roy learned a lot through this process.

After this checking account struggle, Roy could probably empathize with another nester, whose mother wrote, "The other day I was sorting the laundry and some white breath mints rolled out. One of them had some numbers on it. It read, '2376-185.' I asked my son if it was important. He said, 'It's either check number 2376 for $1.85, or check number 185 for $23.76.' Then he shrugged and popped it in his mouth."[6]

The following account is an illustration of a checking account turned nightmare. James, a 27-year-old nester, quit his job with a local utility to start a small business. Rather than open a new account he converted his existing personal account to a business checking account. As with many entrepreneurs, James struggled to make ends meet. He began to bounce checks. Even though he took care to cover each returned check and pay all NSF charges, his bank became concerned. It sent a letter advising him that if he persisted in this practice it would cancel his account. This frightened James sufficiently that he cleaned up his act for a short time. But soon he reverted to his practice of bouncing checks.

The bank made good on its threat and closed his account. Shaken, he went to another bank and attempted to open an account. During the application process the new bank learned of the recent cancelation and refused him. He learned that its policy was a five-year waiting period. Imagine his desperation! It is difficult to operate a business without access to a checking account.

Fortunately for James, he had continued to maintain a small savings account with the credit union associated with his former job. It allowed him to open a companion checking account. This time James read the small print. After three bounced checks in any three month period the new account would be automatically closed. A strict policy, but fair under the circumstances.

The story of James continues. During a chat with his mother he learned that his younger sister, Tiffany, was now bouncing checks. James sat down with her and told her his sad saga. He begged Tiffany to shape up and quit bouncing checks, even recommending she open another small account as a precaution. Tiffany wouldn't listen and within weeks her account was terminated. Luckily, James' credit union allowed family members to join, but it required a one-year waiting period after a forced closure. A full year of costly and inconvenient money orders taught Tiffany the value of responsible checking account usage.

A tip that concerned parents might give forgetful nesters is to order the carbon-backed type of checks. The carbons can help enormously when balancing a checkbook.

ATM's and credit cards

The emergence of automated teller machines (ATM) has had a tremendous impact on our cashless society. This is a service many financial institutions offer their customers as a means of obtaining balance information, making deposits and transfers, and securing cash withdrawals.

The customer is given a card with a secret personal identification number for use in various machines. In choosing a bank that offers this service, it pays to comparison shop. Most banks offer two or more free transactions per month, and the cost for additional transactions can vary widely. A small local savings and loan might offer great personal service but their ATM cards may be used at only a few select locations. Another ATM card from a credit union can be used for deposits and withdrawals at most machines in the area but will not allow the owner to obtain balance information.

Overall, ATMs are a wonderful service but can become dangerous if one does not keep careful track of each transaction. A few cash withdrawals not recorded can be costly. A visitor to any cash machine will find vast quantities of discarded receipts. Caution your nester to save each slip until it is properly noted and accounted for.

Credit cards can be beneficial in establishing credit or can be a disaster. Because of banks' intense competition, most employed nesters and many unemployed college nesters are able to obtain their first credit card relatively easy. In fact, some may feel these cards are being forced down their throats. However, once a card is abused, your nester may find it hard to obtain any credit whatsoever. Again, comparison shopping is wise. Credit limits, minimum payments and interest rates vary widely.

In assisting your nester in establishing credit, you may want to recommend that he or she choose a card that requires payment in full at the end of every month. This enables him or her to build up a positive credit rating without incurring a costly loan balance. Many cards allow a customer to charge cash advances for a fee. Most have procedures available to obtain emergency credit increases. All have charges for late payments. The best advice to a new credit card holder is make all payments on or before the pay-by date, charge sparingly and pay off the entire balance, and not just the minimum amount due, whenever possible.

Taxes

If a person, even a nester, doesn't file income tax returns, he or she will be in trouble with the Internal Revenue Service sooner or later! How is the young person going to learn about the world of taxes? The printed information available is often so confusing and detailed that young people can't or won't read it. Like it or not, our nesters usually learn about the importance of collecting tax data and how and when to file from us, their parents, or from their friends.

But it's not always easy. Like many people, Ann, a 24-year-old nester, has difficulty handling her personal mail. She will occasionally look over her mail pile after work, but unless something looks exceptionally interesting—like an invitation to a party—it just lies on the table, begging to be taken care of. Or, sometimes she picks up her mail, walks to another part of the house where she casually opens the envelope, glances over its contents, and then drops it on the nearest table. With a person like Ann, it's almost a given that when it's time for her to file her income tax forms, she is going to have trouble finding her W-2 records. They are sent out each January to anyone who has earned income the preceding year. A gentle hint from Mom on the day the W-2 arrives to the effect that Ann will need this form to complete her income tax returns, may help in preventing a problem.

There's another tax complication that some nesters, and parents, need to be aware of: tax money is not withheld from the paycheck in certain jobs. It's true for anyone who is a sole proprietor of a business, for some salespeople, and for many household and farm jobs, to name a few. In these cases, nesters should keep records throughout the year so that the figures are available when the time comes to fill out the IRS return. However, it may be necessary to file estimated tax returns four times a year in some of these jobs. So it might be advisable to check with an accountant regarding one's taxes.

Parents also can be helpful to their nesters at the time the parents are working on their own IRS returns. It would be a kindness to show their nesters how the process is done, so that they can be reminded to start compiling their own data for Uncle Sam. While it is appropriate for parents to remind their nesters—especially first-time tax payers—of their obligations, it is best for nesters to gather their own data and fill out their own forms. Or parents can recommend that their nesters take the tax information to a professional tax accountant and pay the fee. It should be stressed that nesters must allow plenty of time to receive professional help before the tax deadline.

Whatever he or she chooses to do, the April 15 deadline may

need to be emphasized. By being responsible for his or her own taxes, the nester will learn the mechanics of the tax system and the cost of this necessary fact of citizenship. He or she must know that there will be a financial penalty from the government if tax returns are not filed on time. An added incentive is the possibility, in some cases, of getting an early refund if the forms are sent in before the rush. If tax forms for a given year are not sent in, the government will keep the money that is withheld from the nester's paycheck to cover the tax and the government files at the highest rate. If not enough money has been withheld throughout the year, the government has the power to seize all funds available in checking and saving accounts—without advance notice—to satisfy the nester's tax bill.

Despite the threat of being called nags, parents should assist their nesters in tax procedures until they get the hang of it. It's a vital part of their financial education.

Budgeting

A good budget is helpful in reaching goals and in planning for emergencies. A nester's long-range goals could include saving enough money for a down payment on a house, which could take years. An intermediate goal could be saving for a good suit, which might take several months. Immediate goals would include items such as rent, car payment, insurance, etc., that have to be paid each month.

Not everyone has the discipline to save and spend money wisely, however. Many people's first reaction to their financial situation is similar to that of Gary, a 32-year-old nester. "The problem with my finances is that I just don't make enough money." Yet, when we look at other young people who are making their salaries stretch, it is clear that most nesters have the ability to save a little out of each paycheck. It is not the amount of money they have at their disposal that makes them successful savers, but the proper allocation of their spending.

One mother relates that her husband says that growing up is a series of cuttings. First, it's the umbilical cord, then the apron strings, and lastly, usually much, much later, it's the purse strings.

One nester who hasn't learned this truism yet is Bill. He periodically moves in and out of his parents' home because he can't seem to make it on his own financially. However, if he could learn the secret of budgeting, he would probably become financially independent. Bill, like other young adults, should set down his long-range, intermediate, and short-term goals. A certain amount should also be allocated for emergencies. Studies have shown that all successful people make lists—lists of daily chores, lists of yearly goals, and lists of life goals. Money matters are no different. Parents should encourage nesters to write down their income. Next, nesters should itemize all expenses for one month and rank each item according to priority. They then need to ask how much they would be able to save and what could they do without.

One advantage of a balanced budget, where outflow does not exceed income, is that goals can be realized! He or she can get that new car, or make a down payment on a house! "In three years since he moved into his parents' Miami house, one 24-year-old music industry reporter has stashed away $6,000, bought a used car with cash and traveled to England on his $20,000 salary. His room and board is $25 per week."[7] A budget that is not in balance means that some goals will not be realized, and bankruptcy may not be far behind. For a nester, the result may mean a continued dependence on his or her parents.

A few simple budget rules

1. *List five year, three year and one-year goals.*
2. *Record current expenditures.*
3. *Estimate savings based on intermediate and future goals.*
4. *List net income.*
5. *Balance income with outgo.*
6. *Maintain careful records of income and expenses, especially cash receipts.*
7. *Review records periodically to make sure that spending is kept within budget.*

Net worth

One benefit of living within your means is an ever increasing net worth. Encourage your nester once a year to fill out a net worth statement. A handy reminder is to make this a part of their annual income tax routine. Completing a net worth chart gives one a financial snapshot. It's fun to watch your bottom line grow.

Yearly Asset Growth Estimate

	Start of year	year end	change
ASSETS			
Current assets:			
Cash on hand & in banks:			
Checking accounts	————	————	————
Savings accounts	————	————	————
Money market accounts	————	————	————
Certificates of deposits	————	————	————
Cashable securities	————	————	————
Other	————	————	————
Life insurance cash value	————	————	————
Fixed Assets:			
Real Estate	————	————	————
Securities			
Mutual funds	————	————	————
Stocks	————	————	————
Bonds	————	————	————
Others	————	————	————
Annuities	————	————	————
Pension & profit sharing:[1]	————	————	————
Personal property[2]	————	————	————
Business ownership	————	————	————
Other[3]	————	————	————
Total Assets	————	————	————
LIABILITIES:			
Mortages & Loans:			
Real estate	————	————	————
Cars	————	————	————
Personal loans	————	————	————
Other	————	————	————
Unpaid bills	————	————	————
Other debts	————	————	————
Total Liabilities	————	————	————
Net apparent yearly asset growth	————	————	————
Less impact of inflation	————	————	————
NEW REAL ASSET GROWTH	————	————	————

1/Includes company sponsored plans, IRAs, SEP Plans, Keogh Plans. 2/ Includes automobiles and other vehicles, boats or other expensive property. 3/ Includes collectible items, gold, etc.

Parents often run into the situation of a nester who needs some extra cash, and the question keeps arising: is it a good idea for parents to help out? Perhaps not always. But sometimes, it may be the only way for a young person, who hasn't been working and purchasing long enough to establish a credit rating, to get ahead financially. Let's look at the pros and cons of lending money to our nesters.

Twenty-year-old Jerry wanted to buy a used car. It was seven years old, in good condition, and would cost $2,500. His folks could easily have lent Jerry the money, but they felt that this was a good opportunity for him to learn how banks operate, and to establish some credit. They advised Jerry to go to the bank for his car loan. This he did and was told he would need a co-signer on the note. His parents agreed to co-sign, making certain, however, that Jerry knew that it was his loan and he would be responsible for paying it back. This way, his parents were able to help him out financially, without having to shell out the cash.

Before you do this, be certain you trust your child in financial matters, since a poor payment history would reflect on your record. Additionally, if the nester defaults on the loan, you should know that you will be responsible for repayment.

Here's an example of a parent who did decide to shell out cold, hard cash. Cheryl, at 25, wanted to buy into a partnership with her two friends. The three women planned to open a specialty shop and needed operating capital to buy inventory. The shop would be in a good location, where there was a need in the neighborhood for a business of this type. It was also evident that they were taking a very business-like approach to the venture, for they had done a complete market analysis. Cheryl didn't have the capital for her share, so she approached her dad. He thought it was a great opportunity for his daughter, and since he had some cash reserves, he was willing to lend her the money. He felt that it would be a good investment, one likely to succeed, and he could see that Cheryl was excited and enthusiastic about the business.

So, he lent her $10,000. They signed a formal agreement, specifying all the terms of the loan, including a repayment schedule and the interest rate. Cheryl's dad believes that ultimately his initial investment will be recouped, with interest. As an added plus, his daughter will make her debut into the business world.

On the other hand, you may want to know about Mrs. Bauer, who illustrates the flip side of this coin. Mrs. Bauer and her husband planned their finances so that they would have a good income upon retirement. However, Mr. Bauer died at age 58 from a heart attack. In addition to their savings, Mrs. Bauer also had her husband's life insurance benefits, which were considerable. She was financially secure.

Before the second anniversary of her husband's death, her 28-year-old nester, Mark, came to her with a sure-fire investment scheme. All he needed was a hefty temporary loan from his mother.

Mark assured her that he would quickly double her investment. His enthusiasm completely discouraged any questions his mother was able to muster, and over the objections of legal counsel, she made the loan her son requested.

Within nine months, it became evident that he would not make the financial killing he had envisioned. Before the year was out, his mother knew that she would never see her money again. This was doubly tragic because not only was his mother without funds (she lost the family home and had to go to work in a department store), but the four other children in the family lost their inheritance as well.

Many business ventures of a similar nature are quite risky despite market surveys and enthusiastic partners. Parents should be cautious about this type of loan, realizing the risk involved. In the event of a business failure and the inability of the nester to repay the loan, a lifetime of bitterness can follow.

Points for a parent to consider before making a loan are:

Business loan considerations

1. *Do the business partners have any managerial ability and experience?*

2. *In case of a joint venture, do partners know that they are personally responsible for partnership debts?*

3. *Have they made realistic sales projections that indicate an adequate profit?*

4. *Have they made arrangements for adequate accounting and tax advice?*

5. *In the event that one of the partners wants to leave the partnership, has a formula been agreed upon as to the amount to be paid by the remaining partners as well as the method and the terms of payment?*

Sometimes the parents' desire to help their offspring blinds them to the risks involved. Unfortunately, too much animosity has developed between relatives or friends whose joint ventures went awry. Yet, if after taking everything into consideration, you still want to lend the money to your nester, more power to you!

Some parents stated various reasons why they have lent money to their nesters:

One mother wrote that her 23-year-old daughter "occasionally needs a loan for a payment that she's behind in—sometimes for a car payment and sometimes for an insurance payment."

A 19-year-old male nester writes that he needs "loans—not gifts—for my social life and clothes."

Another parent relates that her two grown sons have needed loans five times, in amounts of $3,000 or less, for trailer home investments, car purchases, etc. These loans are expected to be paid back as soon as possible.

Some parents who lend funds to several grown children have a revolving account. Often, one offspring will be repaying as another is borrowing. Yet another mother tells us of her 28-

year-old daughter who lives at home and is working full time: "She needs $100 every other month for incidentals until her paycheck comes."

Health insurance

Most people consider health insurance a necessity, but what 21-year-old knows or believes this? They still have that wonderful sense of invulnerability. Often your nester needs to be educated about health insurance. Here is the story of one nester who had to learn the hard way.

Tony, age 21, is a nester who never left home. He is working for a small firm which doesn't have a group health insurance plan. After Tony left school, he was no longer eligible for the family insurance plan that his father carried through his office.

Naturally, Mom and Dad suggested to Tony several times that he should get health insurance. All he would need, they suggested, would be a major medical plan, which shouldn't be too expensive for a healthy young man. They felt he should be covered in case he was in an accident or came down with a costly illness. But Tony didn't want to spend money on something so "non-essential" (in his words) as health insurance.

But one day Tony told his mom that he could no longer tolerate the headaches he'd been having (these headaches were news to Mom) and was going to the doctor. It turned out to be nothing serious, but his trip to the doctor added impetus to mom's encouragement to get health insurance. The next day, when his mom suggested that Tony find an insurance agent, he did. Within a week, he had his insurance policy.

The following month, when it was time to make the second monthly payment on the policy, Tony wrote the policy number on his check and mailed it in. He forgot to include the tear-off section of the policy notice along with the check. He did the same thing the next month.

Soon he received a letter saying that the insurance company

was canceling his account due to non-payment.

They had cashed his checks, but because he had neglected to return the stub, even though the policy number was written on Tony's check, his account had not been credited. Tony had to contact his agent, retrieve his canceled checks, and make copies to prove that he had made his premium payments. Tony learned that while it's important to have health insurance, it's also important to pay attention to how you pay a bill—any bill.

Savings and investments

Though most nesters are living at home because they can't afford their own apartments, nearly all adult offspring remaining at home have many opportunities to save money. A survey for this book, mentioned in the preface, discovered that 52% of nesters do save some money.

Let's look at the features and the benefits of some of the more common methods of bank savings:

Passbook Savings: Safe, easy accessibility, low interest rates, ATMS.*

Interest Bearing Checking Accounts: Accessible, low rates, account fees vary, ATMS. Carbonless-style checks available.

CDs (Certificates of Deposit): Short term, intermediate and long-term availability, rates exceed normal passbook accounts. Safety varies by institution.

IRAs (Individual Retirement Accounts): Long-term savings with tax advantages that vary by individual situations, self-directed or managed investment options. Fees vary considerably.

401Ks (Company Sponsored Retirement Plans): Long-term savings, excellent tax advantages, limited accessibility and investment options. Rollovers and distributions available upon leaving the company.

Keogh Plans: Retirement plans similar to 401Ks for self-employed individuals.

Mutual Funds: Market risk, diversification, multiple investment options, liquid. Choose fee-based or no-load.

Common Stock: Risky, growth potential, income potential, ownership in America, liquid. Choose a full-service or discount brokerage house.

Bonds: Municipal bonds offer income, safety and tax advantages. Corporate and junk bonds offer higher rates, but much more risk.

Real Estate: Long term, tax advantages and tax liabilities, maintenance, market risk. Rental or personal property.

* *Automated Teller Machine Service.*

The bottom line

In dealing with money matters, we must consider what is best for all parties involved—the nester and the parents. Each should ask: What can I do? What am I willing to do?

To answer these questions, one should honestly assess his or her feelings and be open and frank with others about those feelings. Would it be best to give financial aid freely, with no worry of payback? Would it be better to lend money with the expectation of being paid back on a predetermined schedule?

Or would a bank loan (with possibly the parents co-signing) be better? Each situation will be different and must be dealt with separately, carefully and caringly.

In general, however, it seems best for a nester who has an income to pay a percentage of it to his or her parents as room and board.

If the situation is one in which there is no income, or where the nester is saving money, perhaps some work arrangement can be made as a substitute for a monetary contribution.

Through loving concern and communication, most money problems and situations can be worked out in a positive way.

Parents are responsible for the financial training of their children. Likewise, adult children should be committed to growing in financial responsibility. It's a two-way street.

CHAPTER EIGHT

Negative attitudes

"Aren't we a little embarrassed by what the neighbors will think if our kids come home and live with us after college? I mean, if we're such hot parents, and if our kids are so talented, how come they're sleeping upstairs and eating our peanut butter sandwiches?.... There's an attitude that a parent doesn't get the trophy until they're out on their own."
— Television host Phil Donahue[1]

Having a nester in the home can invite negative criticism from our friends, our families, and even from ourselves. We need to recognize how these attitudes influence our actions, so we can relate to our nesters in a positive way.

The opinion of our friends, though subtle, can certainly influence our feelings and thus our actions—especially when we're not quite certain that what we're doing is the right thing. We need to be aware of any negative feelings we're up against, especially if the pressure of our friends' opinions is strong.

On the whole, it appears that today's society is not fully prepared to accept nesting, so we shouldn't be surprised when friends or neighbors make disparaging remarks.

Today the emphasis is on individual success, and some members of society aren't ready to view a nester as a success. Some parents have the impression that other people consider their offspring failures because they aren't living outside the family home.

Friends' comments

The following comments from friends and family (as related in my survey) are typical:

"If you're such great parents, your kids should be independently successful—not still living with you at home." (Some people think one has to leave home to be considered successful. Does this mean that a 50-year-old person who has had a successful career, but lives at home, is still considered unsuccessful?)

"Isn't your kid sponging off you? How can you put up with him at home? These grown kids should be able to stand on their own two feet!" (You and your nester are the only ones who can determine whether he is sponging off you or really needs you.)

"How can you stand living with your parents? Don't they cramp your style?" (By respecting each other as individuals and adults you may actually get along better now than when your young adult was a teenager. Be aware that the comment may, in fact, be prompted by a jealous friend who is not welcome back home.)

"When you leave home, then we'll think of you as an adult, but not before, because when you're out on your own, you'll be forced to take care of yourself and you'll finally really be an adult!" (If this nester paid room and board and helped with the household chores—in short, was a contributing member of the house—possibly his parents would think of him as an adult.)

"You're spoiling your kid by letting him live at home and doing everything for him." (There is a difference between spoiling an offspring and fulfilling a need. Spoiling is when you do things for a person which he or she can do for himself or herself, as opposed to fulfilling a valid need.)

"Those kids are never going to grow up if they continue to live at home." (Just because they live in the parental home doesn't mean that they won't grow and mature. Growth can take place wherever a person lives, if he or she takes responsibility for himself or herself and his or her actions.)

"All 18-year-olds should be out of the home because 20 years ago we were out at that age." (Jobs were more plentiful then; further education not as common, so nesting wasn't such a necessity then.)

"When is she getting married and leaving home?" (This attitude may have come from Colonial times, as the following quote indicates:)

"A girl needed a husband for support, since there was scarcely any work open to her outside the house. The few women who remained without husbands in Colonial days were looked down upon—it was agreed that something must be the matter with them and parents were likely to be embarrassed to have an unwed daughter on their hands. An unmarried woman of 25 was described as a 'dismal spectacle.'

"Unmarried men were not in much better repute. In Hartford, Connecticut, bachelors were taxed twenty shillings a week 'for the selfish luxury of solitary living.' They were expected to report periodically to a magistrate just to make sure they were behaving themselves.

"Puritan New England did not look kindly upon young marriageable males whiling away their time when they could be producing children. This was no place for sowing wild oats."[2]

Times have changed, and thankfully so, but society still has a bit of a hangover from these Colonial times, in that our first impression of an older, unmarried person is often wary or negative.

However, when we stop to think about it, it's really a person's own business if he or she chooses to stay single.

Responses to friends' comments

It may seem an impossible task to change our friends' attitudes. However, it is possible to choose how we will react.

Following are ways that some families have responded to negative comments:

Accept them in silence and become resentful. If we do accept these comments in silence, then emotions can fester and pop out in open resentment toward the nester with such remarks as, "Why don't you get a decent job that pays a living wage? Then my friends will quit bugging me about you!"

Get defensive. "Why don't you mind your own business?"

Ignore them. "I get bad vibes from friends and relations, but I just pay no attention to them. If they don't like it, that's their problem, not mine."

Explain why they are a nesting family. "He or she needs (or wants to) live at home for awhile. Anyway, the family should dictate to society, not vice versa."

Applaud the benefits of nesting. "When I hear disparaging remarks, I tell that person about the positive side of living at home."

If you are being exposed to negative attitudes, it's going to be harder to deal with nesting in your home. So, if you have a nester, the object is to learn to deal with the negativeness positively. Then you can accept and enjoy living together as a family. Here are a few more quick responses for your arsenal:

"I feel this is a special time in our lives and I want to enjoy it."

"I do what I think is right for my family."

"I could move out, but there is no pressure from my parents to go. I'm glad that they let me live at home."

"My daughter seems to appreciate all the things I did for her when she was young, because she is anxious to be helpful to me now that she's grown up."

"If I can't get along with my parents, I won't be able to get along with other people who may have differing attitudes."

"Every family is different and every person is different. Let's live our own lives and let others live as they choose."

"Occasionally our situation gets criticized, but it's mostly by people who don't understand family ties."

"I tell my buddies to compare my bank account to theirs."

"I tell them they're nuts to criticize because I have it so great."

"I try not to worry about it when my friends make negative remarks."

"It's none of their business!"

Parents' attitudes

When parents detect negative attitudes from their friends about their nesting situation, they may begin to have doubts themselves, as the following comments show:

"Whose house is this, anyway? Yours or mine?" (Some families with nesters have a problem with a confrontation of wills. We need to decide whether the nester is a guest, a boarder or an integral part of the family whose wishes, needs and desires are considered.)

"Is this ever going to end? Is he ever going to move out or will he go on living here for the rest of his life?" (If the relationship has deteriorated to this point perhaps it is time for a family conference to iron things out or discuss a target date for moving out.)

"Years ago young people were blamed for the deterioration of the family because they left home. Now when they need to return to that home, some people feel they cannot stand on their own feet." (It seems that no matter what young people do—stay or leave—they will be criticized.)

"I'm a failure as a parent because my kid is a failure." (His son doesn't have a high-paying job and can't afford to live in an apartment. Just because he is living at home for the time being doesn't make anyone a failure.)

"I know what's good for you better than you know yourself." (Some parents have an attitude of infinite wisdom regarding their nesters. This attitude can ultimately stifle growth.)

Nesters' attitude

Some nesters' attitudes prevent them from nesting when it really would be better for them to do so.

"I need to live at home because I can't afford to continue on with school if I have to pay high rent and tuition too. But I blew up that bridge by bragging when I moved out that I could be a big success on my own." (Pride and stubbornness can prevent a nester from rejoining the family in time of need.)

The end result of hearing comments from know-it-all friends or, indeed, our own negative feelings may be that we take out our irritations on our nester, spouse or other children. Or we bury the remarks deep within, where they fester, only to emerge later as a stinging comment aimed at some unsuspecting family member. Disapproving comments may affect a parent or nester so deeply that the nester is no longer able to go on living at home.

A nester's underlying attitude toward home, parents and family will certainly dictate his or her actions. Therefore, it will be helpful to look at situations where nesting has worked out well, and examine the nester's attitude.

One 22-year-old nesting son writes, "I'm glad that my parents let me live at home. I don't wish to move out. I'm financially able, but there is no pressure from my parents to go. I boast to my friends how wonderful and understanding my folks are. We don't have any troubles." Maybe the key word in this son's writing is "let." He realizes that his parents are allowing him to live there; it's a privilege that he appreciates.

One young lady said she felt it was important to know that she was welcome to live in her parents' home. She declined, feeling it wouldn't work out, but it meant a great deal to her that her parents voiced their willingness to have her live with them if she wanted, or needed, to do so.

Another young woman gave this heartfelt statement, "Be it ever so humble, there's no place like my mom's!"

Sometimes it's not easy for the nester to fit into the daily routine in her parents' home, now that she is an adult. Kate, quoted in *Time* magazine, realistically states, "I have learned the hard way not to fight with my parents about my sense of values. I now realize I have to compromise. This is their territory."[3]

A 22-year-old woman wrote, "I am most appreciative of the fact that I can live at home while getting started in a career. However, my need to grow and be more independent will affect the current living arrangements in a short time. I plan to move out soon."

The following two nesters show a wide degree of variance in attitudes.

A 31-year-old female nester wrote, "I'm very happy with the situation. It seems to be a good one. Financially, it's affordable for me and provides a little extra income for my parents. In terms of personal growth, it has given me an opportunity to further my education." (She's working on her master's degree.)

On the other hand, some nesters feel guilty about living at home. Like so many others, they think they shouldn't still be living with their parents.

One 32-year-old nester, in particular, has lived at home with his parents for many years and evidently it has worked out well for him and his family. Yet, he feels guilty about living there. It could be that societal pressure has affected his attitude.

It is clear that there are difficulties in living with nesters because of social attitudes. But if these difficulties are faced and dealt with, then nesting can be a workable and wonderful situation.

Understandably, what nesting families are asking for is a non-judgmental attitude from society, so that they can be free to live as they feel they must.

Certainly, it is better to try to understand other people than it is to criticize them.

Target departure date

It is much easier to have patience with a nesting situation if one knows that there is a termination date.

Yet, only a few families say that they have discussed an expected departure date, such as a wedding, a college entrance or a specific arbitrary target date for the nester to move.

One mother wrote that her nester was planning to leave after he finished school (he was commuting to college while living at home), for then he would be able to support himself.

Some families said that they had "vaguely" discussed the topic, and one nester wrote that his family had discussed a "tentative" departure time.

Another mother mentioned that her nester planned to leave home when the weather was suitable for a move.

One weary mother of nine children (two of them nesters) wrote, "Yes, I have discussed it with them, and I told them anytime was fine with me!!!"

However, some families felt that length of stay wasn't a problem:

"He won't be with us forever—it won't be for much longer."

"They all leave on their own—naturally—when the time is right. It just isn't this daughter's time yet, I guess. I don't understand attitudes of people today. They think when kids get out of high school they must leave home. Why? In order to be independent? They can be independent and still live at home."

"I feel if you raise your child right, there's never any time you're going to have to say, 'You have to leave,' because they'll know when it's time to go."

"Surely the average young adult wants to become independent just as soon as he or she is able and will leave the family home when the need (whether financial or emotional) is no longer there."

"My parents always let us know the door was open, and that we could come home. But they also advised us that our stay would be temporary."

Some parents felt nesting was acceptable for a limited time only.

One mother with a 30-year-old son living at home said, "I think after a certain age it's better for everyone for the offspring to have his own apartment."

Two parents were a little more specific:

"It's okay for them to live at home, but by the late 20s or so, it's getting too extreme."

"By age 25, they should be out and on their own."

So some people think that it's all right to nest for a period of time, but that it shouldn't be for too long.

How long is too long? It's up to the individual families themselves to decide, without influence from friends or relations.

It would seem that a discussion of plans to decide specific or tentative moving dates would ease tensions. This allows parents to see a light at the end of the tunnel and can make life with a nester more pleasant.

Sit down periodically with your nester to discuss his or her plans and goals. This will provide a natural opportunity for you to set up a time-line.

If your nester is living away from home and asks to move back, it is best to discuss an estimated time of departure before he or she moves in.

This conversation is also your opportunity to talk over house rules and expectations.

Power of attitudes

We've looked at attitudes about negative criticism regarding nesting. Recognizing how these attitudes can shape behavior helps people relate to nesters in a positive way.

We've also learned key responses to help deflect the pain of negative criticism and strengthen our resolve to accept nesters, when the need arises.

Additionally, setting a target date for the nester to pull up stakes will help him or her set goals. It will also make the parents feel more comfortable with the idea of nesting.

Marlin

CHAPTER NINE

When nesters choose lifestyles different from their parents'

*"You want to be able to sleep with this girl
in your parents' home?"*
— Television host Phil Donahue[1]

Just what is considered an alternate lifestyle? In one family, it may be smoking cigarettes, and in another, it may be involvement with hard drugs. Some parents react as intensely to the first as another family would to the second. Consider that one father kicked his son out of the family home because of the son's use of hard drugs, while another father dismissed his daughter from the home because she didn't leave for Sunday church service on time.

It is important to realize that it's not always the severity of the action, but the depth of the family's feeling toward that action, that triggers a response. Parental feelings can intensify a problem between them and their nesters, making the situation more difficult to solve. When parents are confronted with a nester who has chosen a life with a different set of values than theirs, the parents usually have difficulties dealing with the situation. They can become perplexed and frozen into inaction because they are unsure of the course of action.

Parents may well be tempted to think that the end of all things is at hand when offspring choose an alternative lifestyle. They are likely to be sure when young people "drop out," scorning the traditional work ethic to live in self-imposed indolent poverty, or when they live in coed college dorms and bring home sexual companions for weekends expecting to share the same bedroom.

Understating things somewhat, sociologist Robert Winch remarks that "This is one helluva time to be a parent."[2]

How society affects our values

Societal norms can affect us deeply, sometimes causing us to change our individual values. This may be for the good, since it can make life easier. We also might be adversely affected and our life can be made more difficult. Yet no matter how tightly the family draws in on itself, the outer world cannot be kept out. It follows the family into the home. Television, radio, books, magazines and newspapers now subject adults and children alike to a flood of external ideas. Most of this broadening of outlook improves the quality of life; it has made people better informed and more sophisticated than ever before. But this great benefit is not achieved without cost. For the mass media's flood of information also transmits the stresses and conflicting attitudes of the outer world into the heart and mind of the family, challenging and often upsetting values.[3]

Some parents give up. Other rant and rave. What's a parent to do? Their nesters may have different sets of sexual values and may insist that, while living at home or during a visit, they be given sleeping arrangements which their parents disapprove. In situations like this, parents are thrust into uncomfortable predicaments. But, it's also difficult for the young people.

"I wasn't really nervous about meeting Cindy's mother," says Nick. "It was her father that scared me. After all, I was sleeping with his daughter; I could almost feel the shotgun in my back."[4]

One nester had a problem with her mother: "I'm 25 years old. I've been married and divorced. When I was married, my husband and I lived with my mom. Now I still live at home. But I'm having a dispute with my mother on who to bring into the house and who to bring into certain parts of the house."[5]

Because of rapidly changing societal values, families are caught in the middle with no firm guidelines on to how to act. By keeping the perspective that love and respect for each other is a fundamental base for our adult-to-adult relationships, it will be easier to explore this topic and come to a workable decision.

Parental love and respect

Can parents still love and respect a nester if he or she chooses a lifestyle not in keeping with theirs? Many parents have wrestled with the knotty problem of how to maintain open communications between themselves and their adult offspring when this happens. Vicky, a mother of 17 children, says she doesn't want to place too much guilt on her children. She tells herself that, if they end up with different values, she might cry for a while, but she won't die over it.[6] That's an advisable attitude to take. It's so easy to think the end of the world has come if our grown children depart from our norms.

We can more easily accept such deviations in other families than in our own. It might help if we look at our children through the eyes of an outsider.

We all know families in which the offspring have chosen to use marijuana, and family relations still continue—life still goes on. Another point to consider if we're upset is why we are upset. Do we fear criticism from our friends, or are we truly concerned about our nesters? Our relationship with our own offspring is much more important than any we can have with our friends.

Counselor Ralph Ranieri feels that grown sons and daughters

"must respect their parents' feelings and customs, but they must also feel free to make legitimate choices that may be contrary to their parents' aspirations."[7]

These choices are a natural part of growing up. Often, after a period of experimenting with this newfound freedom of choice and rebellious stages of varying length, many adult children ultimately revert to their parents' values and lifestyles.   First, parents have to sort out in their own minds just how to relate to an offspring who has branched out beyond their values. How does one go about that sorting? How can we still respect someone if we don't approve of his or her conduct?

Psychologist Howard Halpern gives some insight:

The child thinks he has done something unthinkable, beyond the pale. His punishment for deeply disappointing the parents is not the withdrawal of love, but the withdrawal of their respect. The granting and withdrawal of respect are enormously powerful enforcers. We need to feel that our parents value us as worthwhile human beings, and do not simply love us because we are theirs. We need to feel our parents like us. Parents communicate that if we don't follow their rules, they may still love us, because after all, as parents they should, but they won't like us. And that's heavy.[8]

But, how can we respect our nester if he or she has chosen a radically different set of values than those in which we believe? Halpern gives some further suggestions. Speaking from an offspring's viewpoint, he says:

You have to indicate your discovery that different ways of living— which your parent may have invalidated as the practice of sinners or barbarians—have value in the lives of others because others, like you, are different from him or her. You have to make it clear that you have no desire to have them change the rules they live by because that is what seems right to them. Neither do you need their approval of your choices.   What you would really like is for them to maintain their respect even when you make choices different from those they feel are right.[9]

Two parents were strongly pro-life and they had often conveyed their respect-for-all-life feelings to their sons and daughters. One day while casually opening the mail, mom saw a bill from the local county hospital. Wondering what services this bill pertained to, her calm evaporated when she saw that they were being billed for an abortion. An overwhelming sadness enveloped her when, upon calling the hospital, she discovered that this bill was not in error and concerned services for their 19-year-old daughter who was living at home. The hospital had sent the bill by mistake to their home after the daughter requested that it be sent to her place of employment. Realizing the pressure their daughter had been under, Mom related that she and her husband needed to draw heavily upon their Christian principle of forgiveness when confronting her.

There are many more pressures on young people today than what many parents experienced in our growing-up years, pressures such as:

- Choice of sexual preferences
- Resistance to authority
- AIDS and other diseases
- Trend toward increased leaves from work
- Drug abuses
- Abortions increases
- Inter-racial relationships
- Increase in divorce rate
- Need for advanced education and more years of school

Realistically, how can we expect our young people to react to situations as we once did when they are living under different social pressures than we experienced? We have to give our adult children credit for examining an issue, and making the best decision that they can under the existing restrictions they experience. Then, it becomes their decision. And true, their decision may be different from one we as parents would have made when we were their age. But again, they are living under different conditions than we were. Society is much more open and accepting today than it was 30 years ago. Can't we respect our nesters for having examined the situation and then come to their own decisions without making judgments against them?

If a parent feels that a nester's behavior is wrong, he or she has a right and a responsibility to communicate his or her view to the nester. The parent must make it clear, though, that it's the behavior to which he or she objects—not the nester.

Some nesters make the following plea: "You and I are different, and I respect who you are and would like you to respect who I am."[10]

If our nester has made choices that are working to help him or her live a fuller, happier life, then the end result is that he or she is making choices that are good for him or her.[11] For example, Ted, a 21-year-old student, felt he needed to drop out of school for several months to think about the direction his life was headed. After this sojourn—which appeared to be sheer laziness to his parents—he decided to change his college major. Now he is studying in earnest and is looking forward to working in his chosen field after graduation.

One mother relates this story about her dropout son: After plodding through two years of college, he quit school. He hibernated in their Canadian outback home with his parents. Mom realized that he had been under severe pressure in college and felt he needed a rest. But understanding this didn't stop her from feeling anger every time her son shuffled the cards for yet another game of solitaire. Day after day, month after month, the son continued his card playing. Suddenly after a year, the son announced that he was ready to rejoin life. He re-enrolled in school and left home. Mom, who previously shuddered every time she heard those cards being dealt, now wishes she had stopped her work to play a few games with her son. It had been a special opportunity, in disguise.

Another mother shared her agony upon learning that her son had chosen another male as his sexual partner. These parents had raised four children and felt they hadn't treated this son any differently than the others. However, he confided that while away at college, he came to believe that his orientation was homosexual. It took some getting used to, and many months of real pain, before they could accept their son's companion as part of their holiday family gatherings. Through the information they received from a support group in their community, they learned that research suggests that homosexuality can be a matter of genetics (sexual orientation programmed before birth), breeding (instances which happen during formative years), or choice (freely choosing an alternative lifestyle). These parents came to accept their son's orientation, and Mom and Dad realized that they still loved him as before.

Keeping up parental standards

Some parents have so clearly announced their standards that their nester knows exactly what's acceptable in the home. Even while loving and respecting a nester who lives a different lifestyle, parents can still have house standards. As one mother of a 31-year-old nesting son stated, "This is our house. You are welcome here, but this is what we believe in and that governs what goes on in this house. If you chose to behave differently, maybe you shouldn't live here."

Each parent has a different flash point—various levels where he or she draws the line—and each nester should know where his or her parent's line is drawn on particular issues. The following nester who telephoned into the show received some free advice from television host Phil Donahue:

Phil: "So you want freedom to bring a girlfriend home?"
Young Man: "Yeah, I do, because the lease where we're living is under both of our names, my mother's name and mine."
Phil: "Oh, OK,you want to be able to sleep with this girl?"
Young Man: "Pardon me?"
Phil: "You want to be able to sleep with her?"
Young Man: "I want to be able to have the same freedom I'd have if I were on my own."
Phil: "So, you want to be able to sleep with her?"
Young Man: "Right."
Phil: "Is that right?"
Young Man: "That's right."

Phil: "All night long? Don't you feel any obligation to at least honor your mother's traditional values?"

Young Man: "But I'm honoring her traditional value by paying half of the rent!"

Panel Member: "But you're living under her roof."

Young Man: "I think I'm honoring it by..."

Phil: "Hang on just a moment. I've got some free advice for you. Leave and get your own apartment."[12]

Following is an example of a young person who moved out because of her mother's objections. Tracey said, "When I was 19 years old, I had a boyfriend my mother didn't care for and she gave me a choice. Either stay home and get rid of him, or leave and keep him. So, I left home. Well, he went away to school right after I moved out of the house. So I turned around and moved back home."[13]

The point is that the parents are in charge. It's their house, and they set the standards for the house. If their offspring do not agree with these standards, they are free to move out.

Ways families handle problems

In talking and communicating with other families about cigarettes, marijuana, hard drugs, alcohol and sex, the responses were varied:

Cigarettes. The responses about cigarette smoking were surprising. Only about a quarter of the nesters smoked cigarettes. One nester even wrote, "No, I don't smoke cigarettes! Do I look that stupid?" One mother wrote that her nester did smoke, but that he had been asked not to smoke in the home. The mother said she worried because they have a "No Smokers" household insurance policy.

Nester's smoking was not a problem in some homes because other family members smoked and it was an acceptable thing to do. But in the majority of homes, cigarettes were bothersome to non-smokers. One mother reported that she felt smoking was distasteful to other family members. In one case, the mother had developed lung cancer even though she had not smoked any cigarettes in her entire life—her husband, however, did smoke. So, not only is smoking a bad example for younger siblings, but second-hand smoke can be detrimental to family health. However, some nesters are still permitted to smoke in the home. They didn't ask permission and apparently it never occurred to the parents that they could refuse to let their nester smoke in the home.

Some parents place restrictions on smoking. One father stated that his son can smoke only upstairs in his bedroom. Another nester said that when she wanted a cigarette, she has to smoke outside on the front porch.

Family reactions to nesters' smoking varied from mild to intense. One mother said it was irritating, and another replied that she and other family members strongly disliked the nester's smoking. Another mother said that she permits her nester to smoke in the home, but that she found it very irritating. An important point to bear in mind is that the depth of the family members' feelings should be taken into account, and that there should be open discussion about the topic if it's causing disruption in the family. Rather than let these feelings fester, it's best to talk them out and set house rules regarding smoking.

In one family, there was quite a role reversal—the mother smoked and the nesting daughter didn't like it. Mother wrote, "I smoke, she does not. I'm sure she'd prefer that I not smoke, but I feel it's my house and I'm entitled to more or less do my own thing." If the adult daughter didn't like to live with a smoker, she had the choice to move out.

Marijuana and hard drugs. In spite of the illegality of many drugs, some survey respondents still wanted to communicate their feelings about marijuana and hard drugs. Most parents said that there was no use of drugs by their nesters, many were unsure, some replied that their nester was experimenting with various drugs and, in a small percentage, abuse was a major problem.

As might be expected, emotions were definitely intense on this question. One mother wrote, "When our son was arrested for selling drugs, we nearly died. My husband is a prominent person in our community. People felt sorry for us. Three of our friends came over and asked if they could help us with either money or just friendly support. This meant so very much to us. Other friends hurt us deeply by their condemning attitude. We never did talk about it with our relatives, except some close ones. We made our son work two jobs all summer to pay off the lawyer. He also worked for free for us on Saturdays. He will be on probation for a long time. It's been very hard on the family. It's difficult for us to trust and respect him again."

Another mother stated that her two older children had been involved with hard drugs. The younger children have seen the resulting pain and harm to family relationships, friends, jobs and health. They have said that they aren't going to follow their older brother's and sister's lead.

Other reactions to this problem: "Yes, I smoke pot," says one nester, "but my parents aren't thrilled about it."

"I would assume that she uses drugs," wrote a mother. "As far as I know, it has not affected any other family members. If drugs are really being used, I would guess the younger children know it."

"Possibly he uses drugs. That might account for his mood swings that I notice and which definitely have affected other family members."

"Yes, he uses drugs. The rest of the family thinks he's a bum."

"Yes, she's used them in the past. I don't know to what extent. Everyone knows it hasn't been for the best."

If a nester uses marijuana or hard drugs, it generally affects the other family members. In these cases, the family has to decide how to handle the situation. And handle it they should. Family intervention, Narc-Anon, Coke-Anon, or Al-Anon are all avenues for help. In more severe situations, the family may need to have the abuser committed. One parent went so far as to call the police on her own child. Ignoring the situation won't make it go away.

Alcohol. Parental responses regarding alcohol showed that about three quarters of the nesters do imbibe. For some of the families in which nesters drink alcohol, this is not a problem, because, as with cigarettes, other family members do likewise. Some families share wine or beer at family meals. In one family where a nester had repeatedly gotten drunk, the family decided to stop buying alcohol and having it in the home—it was just too tempting. However, as with cigarette usage, whether moderate or abusive, this can cause problems depending upon how the families react.

Some parents felt drinking set a bad example to younger siblings. Other parents worried about drunk driving. One mother was concerned about drinking, because all her children have extremely low tolerances for alcohol. Another parent wrote that her nester's drinking caused tension in the home. A third parent wrote that both her nesters drank beer and she personally felt that it was the same kind of a drug problem as marijuana, in that the end effects were similar. One nester wrote that yes, he drank and, yes, his parents worried, but they trusted his judgment not to abuse alcohol.

A nester wrote, "I use alcohol, not abuse it, therefore my family need not worry." The parents of this nester are happy that he never has abused alcohol. Still, they do have some concern about him because they know that a person's driving ability is impaired after a few beers. And this nester stops at the local bar every Friday afternoon with the rest of the guys on his crew.

Sex. Most parents have heard the wail, "But everyone's doing it!" and studies support it. A 1989 survey reported that 66% of American females have experienced sex before their 20th birthday. In another survey, this one in 1991, involving those 15 to 19 years of age, 97% of females were unmarried and 99%

of the males were unmarried. The study averaged out the four years and found that 53.2% of females in that age group were sexually active and 60% of the males were also. As ages rose, the percentages rose, i.e. at age 15, the percentages were 38.47% of females and 33% of males. At age 19, 75% of females and 86% of males were sexually active.

Well, families I communicated with indicated otherwise. A little less than a quarter of the nesters themselves or their parents indicated an involvement on the part of the nester in sexual activity, while a little less than half replied negatively. The rest were unaware of their nesters' sexual activities or preferred not to respond to this topic. In some segments of the population then, I believe, premarital sex is not the norm.

The deadly disease called AIDS has dramatically changed our world and lifestyles. The rigid morality of the '50s led to the free love of the '60s, herpes in the '70s and AIDS in the '80s and beyond. The fear of AIDS is a contributing factor to many nesters moving back home. These young people don't feel as comfortable moving from one "live-in" situation to the next and so return to the safety of their parental nest.

"Safe sex," unfortunately, is a very misleading phrase. Condoms may be safer than unprotected sex, but the only true safeguard against AIDS is abstention and or monogamy. Old-fashioned chastity is the buzz word of the '90s.

One writer felt that if parents demonstrated affection more openly with their children and their mate, and tried to understand the pressure for sex from their nesters' point of view, some of the problems relating to premarital sex could be alleviated. She writes:

"Affection: One reason sex has become such an explosive issue is that, despite all the talk, adults in America are quite reluctant to express affection openly. So sex becomes this big mystery that goes on someplace in secret.

"Now I don't advocate parents acting out sexually in front of

children. Far from it!

"But I do know it is healthy and produces good attitudes to...hug your children, kiss your mate. Show that mature adult affection is a wonderful thing, and sex is only part of it. This is the healthy context in which we want children to see sex."[14]

One man of 27 claimed no sexual involvement. "I haven't met the right girl yet," he said. One mother replied that she didn't know if her nester was involved in a sexual relationship; she went on to say, "It's none of my business."

One young son, newly fortified with his high school diploma, came to his folks very agitated. "What's the problem?" asked his dad. He sorrowfully replied, "My girlfriend's pregnant. We want to get married!" "That's quite a dilemma," Dad stated, "what about your college plans? How are you going to support a wife and child and still get a degree?" "I'll just have to get a job," the dejected son replied, "and forget about college. That's my new responsibility now."

Later, Mom and Dad talked it over. Realizing that their son had always done well in school and knowing that he wanted to get a degree in business, they came up with a plan. Inviting the young couple for supper one night, they presented their idea. "We'll fix up an apartment for you in the basement, and you can live here rent-free. However, this offer is good for only as long as you stay in college. If you drop out of school, you have one month before you start paying rent or move out." The young people thanked his folks, and accepted the offer.

Now, five years later, he has his degree and a job; they also have their own apartment. Mom and Dad feel good that they've helped the young folks over a rocky period. It certainly wasn't easy sharing space—lots of wrinkles had to be ironed out. An additional benefit, besides knowing they had helped out, is that the new grandparents are especially close to this grandchild, whom they daily saw grow from infancy to kindergarten.

A young woman said that, yes, she had a sexual relationship with her boyfriend, but that her parents didn't know of it. "This is my life, my responsibility. Sex was/is never discussed with my parents." Another nester replied with a tongue-in-cheek response to the question, "Does adult offspring engage in sexual activity?" with, "Only when offered." And yet another wrote, "Not at home."

One husband and wife, as related by the wife, planned to go out for an evening of cards with friends. Their nesting 21-year-old daughter had made separate arrangements to meet her friend for a movie. Because the daughter's car had not been running properly, dad offered to switch cars for the evening to see if he could ascertain the problem. Throughout the evening Mom noticed that her husband was unusually quiet. Generally he was a lively conversationalist.

Upon arriving back home and after they were settled into bed for the night, Dad asked Mom if she wanted to know what he accidently found in the back seat of their daughter's car. "Sure," Mom nonchalantly replied, never dreaming what she was asking for. "Contraceptive supplies," responded Dad. "There was a bag on the floor," he apologetically continued, "and without thinking I looked inside." Mom related that she lay there in shock for some time. Finally, Dad asked her how many times she was going to say that. Mom said, "I didn't say anything, did I?" "You've said, 'huh' seven times now."

Their daughter had been dating an older fellow for almost a year, but they hadn't realize just how serious their relationship was. What to do now? The couple finally decided that it was a decision their adult daughter had made. Although they didn't agree with the path she had chosen, they could still love and respect her as their daughter.

The most difficult aspect of premarital sex for families is when unmarried nesters wanted to engage in sex in their parents' homes, even though it was against parental values. In a very few cases, sexual relations of unmarried nesters was not a problem because it was not against parental values. One nester whose mother did not object replied that "privacy is a problem occasionally—but it would be with any roommate."

In one blended family, second marriages with children from both spouses in the home, mom/stepmom was first dismayed and then angered when upon getting up at night for a bathroom trip she saw female shoes outside her stepson's closed bedroom door. Fuming, she confronted her husband the following morning stating she disapproved not only because the situation offended her moral standards, but that she was concerned that it would set a bad example for her own younger children. The husband replied that he and his sons had an agreement that such a situation was allowed as long as the overnight visitor was gone before breakfast. For peace to return, first this couple had to agree, and then the children in the blended family had to be informed of any changes in values in the home.

Another problem was mentioned by a mother of two nesters, a son and a daughter. Both were sexually active, but it was only infrequently and discreetly for the son. However, the daughter was sexually active often and with no discretion. This was very hard for her parents to handle. Another mother wrote that the family is aware that a nesting son is sexually involved with his girlfriend and that their activities definitely embarrass the teens in the home, who believe it's wrong.

Love, in spite of differences

If nesters choose a lifestyle different from that of the parents, this can cause problems that should be dealt with frankly and openly. These problems need to be discussed, clarifying for both parties the expectations each hold.

Parents can still love and respect their nesters for themselves, in spite of a difference in lifestyle. Respect for the other person can come only when there is an attitude of "I don't like what you do. Yet, I see you've chosen what you think is best for you, and I still accept you and like you as a person."

CHAPTER TEN

Reroosting: dealing with returning nesters

"Parents of grown children tell me their children don't need door keys anymore; they need a revolving door. They're in when they're out of work, out of money, out of socks, out of food and in debt. They're out when they're in love, in the bucks, in transit, in school, and have outgrown their need for milk."
— Humor columnist Erma Bombeck[1]

Not only are grown offspring staying in the family home, but many who had left are returning. More and more parents are seeing their homes fill back up again—homes that they thought they had all to themselves because at one time their children had all grown and left. Parents are remodeling basements, garages and spare bedrooms for these returning offspring. In one New York suburb, so many families were illegally renovating their homes to accommodate married offspring with their families, that the town finally made these two-family dwellings legal.[2]

One man in Massachusetts feels that even many of the college graduates in his town are returning. A businessman from heavily "reroosted" Cambridge says, "These are the children of academics who floated through school, majored in Renaissance literature and find there aren't any jobs for humanities students. They know a good deal when they see it—full refrigerator, a TV, a bed—and so home they come."[3]

However, it's not only college graduates, but also students, working offspring, and out-of-work sons and daughters who are returning home.

Some returnees come home to re-establish ties with the family: One young man, after graduating from college, moved out of state and stayed away for five years. Then he decided to go on to law school; but before he did, he wanted to spend several months at home. "It was important to me to get back in touch with my parents, to let them know what I was doing. I was about to live much farther away from home, to make a serious commitment to a career. It was just very important for me to make my family a part of that."[4]

One mother wrote of her returning daughter, "When she became engaged she moved back home eagerly and seemed to enjoy a renewal or reconciliation with the family. It was as if she realized that her rebellion during the early teen years had been ill-advised and finally she appreciated what had always been available to her. Since her marriage, she and her spouse have shown a need to visit both their families' homes, although they live in their own apartment. The family home seems to generate a much-needed sense of security and belonging."

It's a comforting feeling for grown offspring to know that they're welcome at home. Nesters want parents there as a home base to return to in time of need. "Even after moving out, it is important to feel there's a home to return to if the going gets tough."[5]

Disadvantages of reroosting

Besides the obvious difficulty in learning how to live together again, there are often other disadvantages of returnees, especially recurrent returnees. The emotional upheaval can be draining to both parents and offspring.

A neighbor related how painful it was for her when her son kept moving in and out. "I wept and wailed for weeks the first time my son moved out. I didn't cry nearly so long when he left the second time, and even less the third time... Finally, the sixth time he moved out I said, 'You're not coming back, are you?'" It is also just plain hard work to keep continually moving furniture back and forth.

Repeatedly moving grown children from one place to another was also hard on the following family, which just had helped their 21-year-old son get settled into a house that he was sharing with three buddies. They were all starting another year at the university. But, just two weeks before that, the whole family had also helped an older daughter move from an apartment into a school dorm. Katie, their 15-year-old daughter, sighed, "When it's time for me to move in a couple of years, the family is going to be so tired of moving people that they won't want to help me!"

Another father said that his daughter was in the habit of moving frequently—sometimes as often as every two weeks. His family, too, was getting tired of all the moving. At some point, parents must put their foot down and say, "Enough is enough! Get settled some place and stay there for a while!"

One of the biggest physical disadvantages of having returnees is that they bring their stuff with them—boxes of books, stacks of furniture, racks of clothes, bikes and all types of recreational equipment, kitchen utensils, and towels. Returnees want to keep it safely stored away while they are rerooting. Then they can take it all with them again when they move the next time. The family is somehow expected to find room. One newly married son built a section of shelves in his parents' basement to store wedding presents while he and his new bride lived abroad for a year.

Some things don't take much room, but they can be disturbing, nonetheless. In the authors's family, Patrick, a college student who returned home for the summer, brought along Zebineazer T. Regalo. Who was Zeb? His pet tarantula! Why the fancy name? "Well," he explained, "Zebineazer is his first name. He just looked like a Zeb. 'T' stands for tarantula, and I chose 'Regalo' for his last name because that means 'present' in Spanish and he was a gift from my buddies for Christmas. Simple, huh, Mom?" Some of the family members were quite upset at the thought of having a pet like Zeb in the house!

The situation of a returnee has a different effect than if the nester had just continued to live on in the home after he or she reached 18. Fitting back into daily family life after having experienced independent living usually is difficult.

For example, one reroosted nester, when he lived outside the parental home, had gotten used to freedom from parental supervision, not having to show consideration for other members of the family, being able to smoke in his own place, cleaning only when he chose, and being able to keep any hours he desired.

Parents, on the other hand, have become used to not being involved in their grown offspring's day-to-day existence, to having extra space and privacy in the family home, and not having to share the bathroom. "Long-awaited vacations or a move to a smaller, cheaper place may have to be postponed, and those who've enjoyed peace, quiet and exclusive bathrooms may shirk from the sudden invasion of privacy. Others fret over the diet, romantic activities and phone calls of 25-year-olds as though they were 12 again. You find yourself listening at night for the car to come back, wondering if your son's okay."[6]

"It takes a group of very mature people to make it work," says Ruth Neubauer, a marriage therapist in Yonkers, New York. "Old conflicts are awakened and many parents just carry on being parents, taking over the grandchildren and shaking their heads at new ideas. It's difficult to let children make their own mistakes when you are all under the same roof."[7]

It's not easy to assimilate grown children back into the household. "The big problem...is that nobody quite knows what to expect and how to behave. Therefore, all are proceeding with great caution, continually on the alert about each other's idiosyncrasies and needs, if only to avoid outright conflict."[8]

Other children in the family learn they must make some adjustments in their lifestyle, when a sibling returns home. They may be bossed around by the rerooster and will probably share a bathroom and maybe even a bedroom again. They are required to take phone messages (and get scolded if not taken properly). A 27-year-old laid-off secretary who returned home advised her family, "A proper message includes: caller, callee, date, time, note and name of the message taker. I expect that *all* my calls will be so recorded. Is that clear?"

The following example illustrates the difficulty that can arise between a rerooster and a sibling. Jill, a 20-year-old returnee, was having a loud, heated quarrel with Stan, her 17-year-old brother, about the family car. He had gotten a driver's license after Jill moved out and enjoyed nearly exclusive use of the second automobile.

Now that his sister had returned home, they were having problems sharing the car. Both wanted to use the vehicle one Friday night. Stan didn't want to fight, so he fled to the bathroom and locked the door. Jill wasn't finished with her tirade against him, so she pursued him down the hall and hollered at him through the locked bathroom door. This got no response, so she kicked the door. She apparently kicked it harder than she thought, or the door, which was hollow, was more fragile than she realized—for she felt the toe of her shoe going right through the outer layer of the door!

While quick-to-anger Jill has a lot to learn about compromise and communication, all nesting families have to learn many things over again when an adult offspring returns home. But in most families, points of conflict can be discussed, each one's priorities stated and a settlement negotiated.

One friend mentioned that her daughter had made an observation regarding reunited families. "Large families seem to have their most difficult children coming home more often, while the achievers are doing just fine on their own."

These nesters apparently return because they have difficulty getting along with the outside world—as well as their family. The old adage, "The more difficult it is to love an unlovable child, the more he or she needs that love," is very true!

Advantages of reroosting

The positive side of reroosting is that nesters generally have a new appreciation for the benefits of living at home. Hopefully, they no longer take meals, laundry and cleaning for granted. Once young people have been out of the home and on their own, they really appreciate having these things done for them—at least when they first return! Also, parents now can view their nesters as adults much easier than if they had lived at home continuously. "When you've been on your own for a number of years and you and your parents have gone your separate ways (no matter how much you keep in touch), you begin to treat each other as adults."[9]

Mark Twain once remarked, "When I was a boy of fourteen, my father was so ignorant, I could hardly stand to have the old man around. But when I got to be twenty-one, I was astonished at how much he had learned in seven years."

What a great quote to express how nesters/reroosters come around to seeing their folks as reasonable, and "neat" people. And while the young adult develops more respect for his or her parents, the process works to his or her benefit too. "Your independence is taken for granted at last, and you and your parents finally balance on the seesaw. 'It isn't a question merely of the young person's becoming independent,' says Tilla Vahanian, a New York psychotherapist. 'It is mutual, with both parents and children knowing how to establish the right distance.'"[10]

During reroosting, parents and nester can start off on a new foot and gain a closer relationship (if parents can overlook certain drawbacks such as pet tarantulas!).

Another advantage of having a returnee is that, when he or she asks to move back, you have a perfect opportunity to lay down some solid ground rules.

Helen, a rerooster, said she appreciates having a live telephone answering service now that she has returned home, rather than her answering machine. Previously when she was out, many of her callers hung up without leaving a message. Now, when she is out of the house, there is generally someone around to take messages for her. No more wondering who called without leaving a message.

A mother of a rerooster writes, "It's rewarding for us to see how our son has matured, accepted responsibility and become more aware of others. It gives me a wonderful feeling to see him appreciate home more and no longer take its comforts for granted.

Her son adds, 'It's good to be here,' 'It felt good going to church with you,' and 'I'm sure glad the family went camping together this summer.' There were times during his high school years when time spent with his peers, an important part of anyone's life, seemed much more appealing than attending family outings. He now appreciates his friends, parents, siblings and even his parents' friends for what each has to offer."

The author's daughter, Maureen, who was a recurring rerooster, had a few comments about returning home: "As I was leaving my parents' home the first time (when I had a bedroom upstairs) my sisters were almost selling lottery tickets to see who would get my room. Thank goodness, though, I've never heard mom and dad say, 'No room at the inn' whenever I've said I wanted to come back. But each time I move home it gets a bit trickier. Once you leave, your spot is up for grabs. You learn to be crafty. The last time I came back, all the regular bedrooms were full, so I fashioned myself a spot in a corner of the recreation room. I had a couple hazards to watch out for.

Between the pool cues and the arms of the Foosball table, it was much like an obstacle course. The day started off by seeing if I could miss bumping my head on a foos arm or tripping over a cue stick as I got up out of the roll-away bed. This is not to mention the problem of where to dress, since there was no door on the rec room and two of my brothers had to walk through it to get to their bedroom. After I moved again, my vacant spot in the rec room remained empty until my brother moved back from college bringing his tarantula with him. No one wanted Patrick for a roommate because Zeb, his pet, took up a corner next to his bed!"

My husband and I have always welcomed guests into our home for dinner or overnight. Possibly this practice made us open to the idea of sharing our roof with our adult children. The following stories illustrate life with a full nest:

"I feel that my parents were able to accommodate us adult children at home," daughter Maureen continues, "in part, because they had plenty of practice having other people staying at our home. Many times during my childhood, our house was filled with strangers. At least, they were strangers to me. My folks have always had a soft spot for anyone who needed a place to stay. Vicki, my away-from-home roommate, had car problems one summer when I was back in the nest. Because she worked just down the road from my place of employment, I offered her a ride to work. For convenience, she stayed overnight.

That night stretched into three weeks because she couldn't afford to get her car fixed right away. After about two weeks, my brother Tom finally noticed her frequency around the house. He asked Vicki, 'Have you moved in too?' At the same time, we also had two cousins from Denver staying for several weeks. Plus, my married brother and his wife had just moved out after a one month stay between apartments."

The author's uncle, married but childless, has a favorite story about temporarily staying over at our house. Waking up one morning and wanting to use the bathroom, he listened to the hallway traffic zoom past his bedroom door. He kept waiting for a lull in the bathroom use so that he could get a turn. But people kept flowing in and out of that bathroom. Finally, just as he was getting desperate, there was a vacancy, so he dashed in. No sooner had he locked the door than one of the older children, who was late for work and thought there was a sibling inside, started pounding on the door, shouting, "Hey, you know no one is supposed to lock this door!" (The house rule regarding the second bathroom, made by the kids themselves, was that it shouldn't be locked. To get more use out the this bathroom at prime time, a room divider had been purchased to partition off the stool. We did have another bathroom off the master bedroom for complete privacy.) Poor Uncle Marvin! He hasn't gotten over the shock of mornings at our house yet. He sighed, "No wonder the hallway carpet is wearing out. You've got more traffic here than at a Howard Johnson motel!"

Once we got over the embarrassment of having Uncle Marvin yelled at, we could laugh at ourselves. He's enjoyed telling the story more than once. Having guests and nesters around the house does add spice and humor—if only we remember to look for it.

Surrogate parenting

One mother relates that a long-ago hospitality has been passed on in recent times. Ten years ago, Ellie needed a temporary haven, which she found in the home of a loving aunt. Ellie is now a single parent of an 6-year-old son and operates a daycare business in her home. Additionally, she is now housing her 18-year-old nephew.

This young man had troubles with his stepfather and needed a place to roost. He tried moving in with his birth father and new wife, but that didn't work out, either. Ellie, hearing of his troubles and remembering her time at her aunt's home, welcomed this nephew into her home.

He's now working two part-time jobs, is investigating further education and is saving money for a car. In Ellie's instance, having her nephew stay with her adds adult companionship which she wouldn't normally have as a single parent. Plus, she is rewarding her aunt's kindness by passing it on to another.

"Ma! A-a-h Ma? Bob's here," my son hollered up the clothes chute next to his basement bedroom, when he heard my husband and I return home after a day of visiting Grandpa 80 miles away. As I stuck my head into the top of the chute, I quickly caught on to the hesitant, questioning tone in my son's voice. I asked, "Bob? How long is he here for?" Joe knew that I had understood him correctly for he shouted back up, "Uh, until he and his dad get things worked out. OK?" I glanced at my husband, who was listening to this exchange, saw him nod in the affirmative, and called back, "Sure."

It had happened again—another parent/child conflict that needed a temporary cooling off period. I took a deep breath and knew we were in for another haul; hopefully, this one would be briefer.

Mary and others came to mind. She had stayed for three weeks, Jim for seven weeks, and Eddie, who comes and goes every once in a while, for a few days at a time. Our son had also needed a similar refuge for a few days and a daughter for six weeks. I was glad to be able to show my gratitude to the two families who had succored our children by helping other young people in a like manner.

It seems that independent, hair-triggered, high-powered parents beget like offspring. This parent/offspring combination seems to be a perfect set-up for conflict, especially when the offspring reach those tumultuous, rebellious years.

Since each family operates and interacts a bit differently, it's difficult to fit into someone else's home. Thus, as each day goes by, the separated person begins to realize that her home, her parents, and her situation really aren't that bad; in fact, they often begin to look downright appealing. That's when the phone calls start going back and forth.

Sometimes it takes a few days, sometimes it takes a few weeks, but sooner or later, each of the nine young people whom we personally knew in this situation were reunited with their families.

Here are some of the courtesies I wish I'd known when this first started happening. As these visitors kept appearing at our doorstep, I had questions: Should I call the family? Did they know where their family member was? Would they be embarrassed? Would I feel badly for them? What happens if the individual needs money? What kind of guidelines are needed? Can a target date for leaving be established? Is the newcomer a visitor or should he or she be treated like family? Does the person share in household chores, eat with the family, and have a curfew? What happens if he or she has a job and no car? Does he or she need a ride to and from work or, God forbid, does he or she need my car? Where is the line between charity and common sense?

Surely, there had to be some clearly understood guidelines. In time, these evolved. First, we ascertained our newcomer's needs—be it a safe haven, funds, transportation for work, or a mediator. We also established a target departure date, chores, and house rules.

When someone having family difficulties moved in, we treated him or her as one of our own in regard to duties, obligations, needs and privileges. If not already done, we informed his or her family about his or her whereabouts—to assure them that he or she was safe. Communication is strongly suggested so that the situation can be resolved as swiftly as possible.Often, all that is needed is a brief cooling-off period, a few phone calls between the feuders, and perhaps a meeting.

If you are an optimist, you can enjoy some of the benefits of surrogate parenting: There is the obvious, happy glow one gets from helping out in a crisis. Additionally, the visitor is usually so grateful that he or she often helps out wherever he or she sees a need. In gratitude, one young man installed a much-enjoyed power showerhead in the family bathroom. He still occasionally pops in for a cup of "Mom's" homemade cocoa.

One mom wrote that her family used to nest a 29-year-old man, who was a friend of one of her sons. He came to live with the family for several years and moved out only after finally being asked to leave. This mom feels that her children's friends are people God brought into her life to be ministered to and temporarily to become a part of her life. In the friendly nester's case, several years was long enough, however.

Toward more re-roosting

Returning home, especially when offspring have been living independently and successfully for a time, is often a humbling, embarrassing experience. Reroosters have become accustomed to being in charge of their life; when returning to the nest, they often lose this autonomy. However, these nesters are usually most appreciative of being able to come home to regroup.

Nesting has been an unrecognized phenomenon in our day. Many people don't welcome the idea because it can cause tension and be perceived as failure.

Nesters in past centuries and other cultures have shown that this situation is not new. There are numerous reasons why young adults return to the home, such as finances, rebonding, companionship and mending family relationships. They return home because they are out of a job, returning to school, to get married at a later date, or are staying on in the parental home.

Nesters find that families can help in times of trouble; families find that nesting broadens family interests. However, reunited family life is not easy and needs consideration from all involved parties. Nesting can be a step backward or on-going growth, depending on how the situation is handled.

Talking about problems before an offspring moves back home, along with open, on-going communications, can ease problems relating to nesting. Most families have found that if nesters have an income, some money should be paid as room and board. This helps the nester to manage his or her finances so that when the moving date comes he or she has budgeted rent and living expenses into his or her income.

Negative attitudes from friends and relations are not unusual and can be expected. Each year millions of families are sharing the same roof and reaping the benefits of a fuller life.

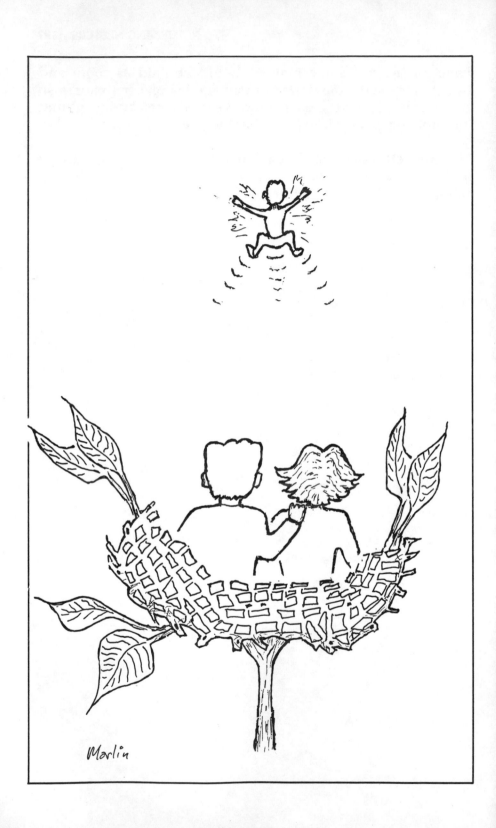

PERMISSION CREDITS

Ann Baker. "The Family That Love Built." *St. Paul Sunday Pioneer Press*, St. Paul, MN. December 14, 1980. Accent Section. p. 1. Used with permission.

Stephen Berg. "How to: Put Up With Your Parents." *Guideposts* Magazine. March, 1991. p. 22. Reprinted with permission from *Guideposts* Magazine. Copyright 1991 by Guideposts Associates, Inc. Carmel, New York.

Sister Kathleen Bierne. "Allow Children to Take Responsibility for Their Mistakes." *Catholic Bulletin* Newspaper. St. Paul, MN. September 1, 1985. p. 13. Used with permission.

Victoria Billings. "Leaving Home vs. Living With Parents." *Glamour* Magazine. June, 1979. p. 100. Copyright 1979 by Conde Nast Publications, Inc.

Andree Brooks. "When Married Children Come Home to Live." *New York Times* Newspaper. New York, NY. January 19, 1981. p. B10. Used with permission.

David M. Brownstone and Jacques Sartisky. *Personal Financial Survival*. Copyright 1981. p. 34 Reprinted by permission of John Wiley & Sons, Inc.

Lorene Cary. "The Return of the Prodigals." *Time* Magazine. October 13, 1980. p. 118. Copyright 1980 Time, Inc. All rights reserved. Reprinted by permission of Time.

Linda Cicero and Steve Sonsky. "A Good Mate is Hard to Find." *The Miami Herald* Newspaper. Miami, FL. February 8, 1981. Sec. G, p.1. Used with permission.

John Cole. "Leaving Home." Reprinted by permission of Blair and Ketchum's *Country Journal*. Copyright February, 1979. Country Journal Publishing Co., Inc.

Nancy Comer and Brie Quinby. "Bringing Your Boyfriend Home." *Mademoiselle* Magazine. November, 1980. p. 200. Copyright 1980 by Conde Nast Publications, Inc.

Michele Cook. "Behind a Cloak of Mystery." *St. Paul Pioneer Press* Newspaper. St. Paul, MN. November 3, 1991. p. 1A. Used with permission.

Phil Donahue Transcript #10280. Air date: November 18, 1980. Courtesy of Multimedia Program Productions, Inc.

Julius Fast. *Body Language*. Copyright 1970 by Julius Fast. Reprinted by permission of the publisher, M. Evans and Company, Inc. New York, NY.

Daniel Goleman. "Leaving Home. Is There a Right Time to Go?" Reprinted from *Psychology Today*. Copyright 1980. Ziff-Davis Publishing Company.

Ellen Goodman. "Together Again." Boston Globe Newspaper. Boston, MA. November 18, 1980. Editorial page. Used with permission.

Walter and Elaine Goodman. *The Family: Yesterday, Today, and Tomorrow*. Farrar, Straus and Giroux. New York, NY. Copyright 1975. All rights reserved.

Jory Graham. "Friend's Death Means Beginning Anew." *St. Paul Dispatch* Newspaper. St. Paul, MN. April 4, 1981. Copyright 1981. Universal Press Syndicate. All rights reserved.

Sydney Harris. "Parents Aren't Rational about Kids and Here's the Reason Why." *Chicago Sun Times* Newspaper. Chicago, IL. February 6, 1981. Used with permission.

Jack and JoAnn Hinckley with Elizabeth Sherrill. *Breaking Points*. Berkley Books. New York, NY. Copyright 1985. Used with permission.

Richard L. Holman. "Japanese Top Savings List." *Wall Street Journal* Newspaper. New York, NY. November 1, 1991. p. A10. Reprinted with permission of *The Wall Street Journal*. Copyright 1991. Dow Jones & Company, Inc. All Rights Reserved Worldwide.

Shirley Taylor Lambert. *Farm Journal* Magazine. Used with permission.

Langway, Kirsch and Hewitt. "Flying Back to the Nest." *Newsweek* Magazine. February, 1980. Copyright 1980 by *Newsweek*, Inc. All rights reserved. Reprinted with permission.

Peter Laslett. *The World We Have Lost*. Copyright 1965. Reprinted with permission of Charles Scribner's Sons.

Nancy Meanix. "Grandparents Too Soon." *Catholic Digest*. September, 1991. pp. 82-86. Copyright 1991 by Nancy Meanix. Used with permission.

Thomas More. *Thoughts for Christian Living* Brochure. Copyright 1976. Eternal Word Television Network, Inc.

Janice Morse and Helen McKinnon Doan. "Adolescents' Response to Menarche." *Journal of School Health*. November, 1987. p.385. Copyright 1987. Reprinted with permission of *Journal of School Health*.

Ralph Ranieri. "Talking It Over—Family Style." *Liguorian* Magazine. December, 1981. pp. 11-15. Reprinted with permission from *Liguorian*.

"For Wilson, Writing Wrap Should Be A Snap." *St. Paul Pioneer Press* Newspaper. St. Paul, MN. April 2, 1990. p. 2C. Used with permission.

"Children's Attitudes Reflect New Equality." *St. Paul Pioneer Press* Newspaper. St. Paul, MN. November 3, 1982. p. 7D. Used with permission.

Lloyd Shearer. "Rent Variations Across America." *Parade* Magazine. December 1, 1991. Used with permission of Lloyd Shearer in *Parade*.

Joan Berg Victor and Joelle Sander. *The Family. The Evolution of Our Oldest Human Institution*. Copyright 1978. Used with permission of the publisher, The Bobbs-Merrill Company, Inc.

Grace Weinstein. "Declaration of Independence." *Glamour* Magazine. August, 1980, p. 61. Copyright 1980 by Conde Nast Publications, Inc.

Marilyn Wellemeyer. "Hubie Clark's Clan Kicks Up Their Heels.170 *Fortune* Magazine. August 11, 1980. pp. 80-94. Copyright 1980 Time, Inc. All rights reserved.

BIBLIOGRAPHY

Chapter One

1 As cited in Goodman, Ellen. "Together Again." *Boston Globe* Newspaper. Boston, MA. November 18, 1980. Editorial page.

2 Cary, Lorene. "The Return of the Prodigals." *Time* Magazine. October 13, 1980, p. 118.

3 *Marital Status and Living Arrangements: March 1990.* Issued June, 1991. U.S. Department of Commerce. Bureau of the Census, pp. 10 & 11.

4.Harris, Louis. "Good Family Life Tops American Priority List." *St. Paul Pioneer Press* Newspaper. St. Paul, MN. January 2, 1981, p. 1.

5 Azzorone, Stephanie. "You Can Go Home Again." *San Francisco Chronicle* Newspaper. San Francisco, CA. December 17, 1980, p. EE-1.

6 Lasch, Christopher. *Haven in a Heartless World: The Family Besieged.* Basic Books, New York. 1977. p. 5.

7 Aries, Phillippe. *Centuries of Childhood.* Knopf. New York, NY. 1962. p. 411.

8 Ibid.

9 Ibid. p. 25.

10 Goleman, Daniel. "Leaving Home. Is There a Right Time to Go?" *Psychology Today* Magazine. August, 1980. p. 57.

11 Goodman, Ellen.

12 Weinstein, Grace. "Declaration of Independence." *Glamour* Magazine. August, 1980. p. 64.

13 Goodman, Elaine and Walter. *The Family: Yesterday, Today, and Tomorrow.* Farrar, Straus and Giroux. New York, NY. 1975. p. 10.

14 MacKenzie, Robert. "Review: 'I'm a Big Girl Now.'" *TV Guide.* February 21, 1981. p. 32.

15 Ranieri, Ralph. "Getting Along With Adult Sons and Daughters." *Liguorian* Magazine. November, 1980. pp. 44-48.

16 Wernick, Robert. *The Family.* Time-Life Books. New York, NY. 1974. p. 88.

17 Goleman. p. 53.

18 Wernick.

19 Cary.

20 *Phil Donahue Transcript #10280.* Air date: November 18, 1980. Multimedia Program Productions. Cincinnati, OH. p. 33.

21 Ibid.

22 Ibid.

Chapter Two

1 As cited in Kett, Joseph. *Rites of Passage.* New York Basic Books. New York, NY. 1977. p. 127.

2 Laslett, Peter. *The World We Have Lost.* Charles Scribner's Sons. New York, NY. 1965. p. 228.

3 Victor, Joan Berg and Sander, Joelle. *The Family: The Evolution of Our Oldest Human Institution.* Bobbs-Merrill. Indianapolis/New York. 1978. p. 72.

4 Ibid.

5 Laslett, Peter and Wall, Richard. *Household and Family in Past Times.* Cambridge University Press. New York, NY. 1972. p. 306.

6 Laslett. p. 92.

7 Laslett and Wall. p. 370.

8 Ibid. p. 369.

9 Ibid. p. 408.

10 Ibid. p. 372.

11 Laslett. p. 83.

12 Morse, Janice and Doan, Helen McKinnon. "Adolescents' Response to Menarche." *Journal of School Health* Magazine. November, 1987. Vol. 57, No. 9. p. 385.

13 Laslett. pp. 88-89.

14 Russell, Josiah Cox. *Late Ancient and Medieval Population.* Transactions of the American Philosophical Society. Philadelphia, PA. 1958. Vol. 48, Part 3. p. 31.

15 Laslett. p. 90.

16 Wernick, Robert. *The Family.* Time-Life Books. New York, NY. 1974. p. 43.

17 As cited in Saveth, Edward N. "The Problem of American Family History." *American Quarterly* Periodical. 1969. p. 318.

18 Ibid.

19 Victor and Sander. p. 63.

20 Goodman, Elaine and Walter. *The Family: Yesterday, Today, and Tomorrow.* Farrar, Straus and Giroux. New York, NY. 1975. p. 43.

21 Wernick. p. 47.

22 Victor and Sander. p. 48.

23 Rhoads, Geraldine. "WD Doings." *Woman's Day* Magazine. November 25, 1980. p. 18.

24 Victor and Sander. pp. 39-41.

25 Goodman. p. 27.

26 "For Wilson, Writing Rap Should be a Snap." *St. Paul Pioneer Press Dispatch Newspaper.* St. Paul, MN. April 2, 1990. p. 2C.

27 Wernick. p. 109.

28 *Phil Donahue Transcript #10280.* Air date: November 18, 1980. Mul-

timedia Program Productions. Cincinnati, OH. p. 17.

Chapter Three

1 As cited in "Thoughts for Christian Living" Brochure. Eternal Word Television Network. Birmingham, AL.

2 Brooks, Andree. "When Married Children Come Home To Live." *New York Times* Newspaper. New York, NY. January 19, 1981. p. B10.

3 Holman, Richard L. "Japanese Top Savings List." *Wall Street Journal* Newspaper. New York, NY. November 1, 1991. p. A10.

4 Billings, Victoria. "Leaving Home vs. Living With Parents." *Glamour* Magazine. June, 1979. p. 102.

5 Unidentified Phone-in Caller.*Twin Cities Today* Radio Show. Minneapolis, MN. December 10, 1980.

6 Cary, Lorene. "The Return of the Prodigals." *Time* Magazine. October 13, 1980. p. 118.

7 *Phil Donahue Transcript #10280.* Air date: November 18, 1980. Multimedia Program Productions. Cincinnati, OH. p. 36.

8 U.S. Bureau of the Census. *The Statistical Abstract of the United States: 1991* (111th Edition). Washington, D.C. 1991.

9 Cicero, Linda and Sonsky, Steve. "A Good Mate Is Hard To Find." *Miami Herald* Newspaper. Miami, FL. February 8, 1981. Sec. G, p. 1.

10 Ibid.

11 *The U.S. Fact Book.* The Statistical Abstract of the United States Bureau of Census. Department of Commerce, 98th Edition.New York, NY. Grossett & Dunlap, 1978.

12 Cicero and Sonsky.

13 Ibid.

14 Ibid.

Chapter Four

1 Bombeck, Erma. "Grown Children Refuse to Leave Home Permanently." *Daily Camera* Newspaper. Boulder, CO. February 6, 1981. p. 13.

2 Wellemeyer, Marilyn. "Hubie Clark's Clan Kicks Up Their Heels." *Fortune* Magazine. August 11, 1980. pp. 80-94.

3 Ibid.

4 As cited in Baker, Ann. "The Family That Love Built." *St. Paul Sunday Pioneer Press* Newspaper. St. Paul, MN. December 14, 1980. Accent Section, p. 1.

5 Bombeck.

6 Langway, Kirsch, and Hewitt. "Flying Back To The Nest." *Newsweek* Magazine. April 7, 1980. p. 86.

7 Ibid.

8 Meanix, Nancy. "Grandparents Too Soon." *Catholic Digest* Magazine. September, 1991. pp. 82-86.

9 Laslett, Peter and Wall, Richard. *Household and Family in Past Times.* Cambridge University Press. New York, NY. 1972. p. 562.

Chapter Five

1 Harris, Sydney. "Parents Aren't Rational About Kids and Here's the Reason Why." *Chicago Sun Times* Newspaper. Chicago, IL. February 6, 1981. Editorial page.

2 *Webster's Dictionary.* J.J.Little & Ives Co., Inc. New York, NY. 1962. p. 676.

3 *Roget's Thesaurus.* Signet, New American Library, Inc. New York, NY. 1977. p. 247.

4 As cited in Goleman, Daniel. "Leaving Home. Is There a Right Time to Go?" *Psychology Today* Magazine. August, 1980. p. 53.

5 James, Marcia, Simon Fraser University of British Columbia, Canada, as cited in Goleman.

6 Goleman. p. 55.

7 As cited in White, Kate. "On Your Own." *Glamour* Magazine. October, 1979. p. 106.

8 As cited in Billings, Victoria. "Leaving Home vs. Living With Parents." *Glamour* Magazine. June, 1979. p. 102.

9 Weinstein, Grace. "Declaration of Independence." *Glamour* Magazine. August, 1980. p. 61.

10 Goleman. pp. 56 & 57.

11 Ibid. p. 53.

12 *Phil Donahue Transcript #10280.* Air date: November 18, 1980. Multimedia Program Productions. Cincinnati, OH. pp. 40 & 41.

13 Goleman. pp. 53 & 54.

14 Weinstein. p. 61.

15 Comer, Nancy and Quinby, Brie. "Bringing Your Boyfriend Home." *Mademoiselle* Magazine. November, 1980. p. 200.

16 Harris.

17 Brooks, Andree. "When Married Children Come Home To Live." *New York Times* Newspaper, New York, NY. January 19, 1981. p. B10.

18 Weinstein. p. 61.

19 Ibid. p. 64.

20 Koral, April and Glassman, Carl. "Are You Your Own Person or Your Parents'?" *Weight Watchers* Magazine. February, 1981. p. 7.

21 Lambert, Shirley Taylor. *Farm Journal* Magazine. Date unknown.

22 Ranieri, Ralph. "Getting Along with Adult Sons and Daughters." *Liguorian* Magazine. November, 1980. p. 47.

23 Ibid. pp. 45 & 46.

24 White, Kate. "On Your Own." *Glamour* Magazine. October, 1979. p. 106.

25 Graham, Jory. "Friend's Death Means Beginning Anew." *St. Paul Dispatch* Newspaper. St. Paul, MN. April 4, 1981.

26 As cited in Weinstein, Grace. "Declaration of Independence." *Glamour* Magazine. August, 1980. p. 64.

27 Bombeck, Erma. "Kids Grow Up Only When Their Parents Permit It." *St. Paul Pioneer Press* Newspaper. St. Paul, MN. June 14, 1981.

28 "Children's Attitudes Reflect New Equality." *St. Paul Pioneer Press* Newspaper. St. Paul, MN. November 3, 1982. p. 7D.

29 Bierne, Sister Kathleen. "Allow Children to Take Responsibility for Their Mistakes." *Catholic Bulletin* Newspaper. St. Paul, MN. September 1, 1985. p. 13.

30 Donahue. p. 25.

31 Cook, Michele. "Behind a Cloak of Mystery."*St. Paul Pioneer Press* Newspaper. St. Paul, MN. November 3, 1991. p. 1A.

32 Hinckley, Jack and Jo Ann with Sherrill, Elizabeth. *Breaking Points.* Berkley Books. New York, NY. 1986. pp. 314-321.

33 Goleman. p. 60.

34 Cole, John N. "Leaving Home." Blair and Ketchum's *Country Journal* Magazine. February, 1979. pp. 77-81.

35 Donahue. p. 19.

36 Langway, Kirsch, and Hewitt. "Flying Back to the Nest." *Newsweek* Magazine. April 7, 1980. p. 86.

37 Koral and Glassman. p. 7.

38 Ibid.

39 Ibid. p. 8.

40 National Institute of Health study, as cited in "Leaving Home. Is There a Right Time to Go?" p.59

41 Ibid.

Chapter Six

1 "Quotable Quotes." *Reader's Digest* Magazine. Vol. 122, No. 732. April, 1983. p. 59.

2 Fast, Julian. *Body Language.* M. Evans & Co. New York, NY. 1970. p. 16.

3 Ibid. p. 10.

4 Ibid. p. 51.

5 Ibid. p. 82.

6 Ranieri, Ralph. "Talking It Over--Family Style." *Liguorian* Magazine. December, 1981. pp. 11-15.

7 Berg, Stephen. "How to: Put Up With Your Parents (Without Being

Put Out of the House)." *Guideposts* Magazine. March, 1991. p. 22.

8 *Vital Statistics of U.S. Government.* Department of Health and Human Services. Washington, DC. 1976 & 1977.

9 *The National Data Book.* U.S. Bureau of the Census. Statistical Abstract of the United States 1991: (111th Edition). U.S. Department of Commerce. Table No. 261, p. 157 and Table No. 634, p. 385.

10 Baker, Ann. "The Family That Love Built." *St. Paul Sunday Pioneer Press* Newspaper. St. Paul, MN. December 14, 1980. Accent, p. 1.

11 Ibid.

12 Wernick, Robert. *The Family.* Time-Life Books. New York, NY. 1974. p. 113.

13 Baker.

14 Brooks, Andree. "When Married Children Come Home To Live." *New York Times* Newspaper. New York, NY. January 19, 1981. p. B10.

15 Baker.

Chapter Seven

1 Wernick, Robert. *The Family.* Time-Life Books. New York, NY. 1974. p. 43.

2 *Phil Donahue Transcript #10280.* Air date: November 18, 1980. Multimedia Program Productions. Cincinnati, OH. p. 17.

3 Ibid. pp. 2 & 3.

4 Cary, Lorene. "The Return of the Prodigals." *Time* Magazine. October 13, 1980. p. 118.

5 "Rent Variations Across America." Intelligence Report. *Parade* Magazine. December 1, 1991

6 Bombeck, Erma. "Youth World Runs on a Small $2 Check." *St. Paul Sunday Press* Newspaper. St. Paul, MN. June 7, 1981. Accent Section. p. 9.

7 Cary.

Chapter Eight

1 *Phil Donahue Transcript #10280.* Air date: November 18, 1980. Multimedia Program Productions. Cincinnati, OH. p. 34.

2 Goodman, Elaine and Walter. *The Family Yesterday, Today and Tomorrow.* Farrar, Straus and Giroux. New York, NY. 1975. p. 77.

3 Cary, Lorene. "The Return of the Prodigals." *Time* Magazine. October 10, 1980. p. 118.

Chapter Nine

1 *Phil Donahue Transcript #10280.* Air date: November 18, 1980. Multimedia Program Productions. Cincinnati, OH. p. 31.
2 Wernick, Robert. *The Family.* Time-Life Books. New York, NY. 19-74. p. 108.
3 Ibid. p. 116.
4 Comer, Nancy and Quinby, Brie. "Bringing Your Boyfriend Home." *Mademoiselle* Magazine. November, 1980. p. 266.
5 Donahue. p. 30.
6 Baker, Ann. "The Family That Love Built." *St. Paul Sunday Pioneer Press* Newspaper. St. Paul, MN. December 14, 1980. Accent Section. p. 1.
7 Ranieri, Ralph. "Getting Along with Adult Sons and Daughters." *Liguorian* Magazine. November, 1980. p. 45.
8 Halpern, Howard. *Cutting Loose.* Simon and Shuster. New York, NY. 1976. p. 105.
9 Ibid. p. 114.
10 & 11, Ibid.
12 Donahue. pp. 31 & 32.
13 Ibid. p. 11.
14 Winship, Beth. "Balancing the Voices Saying, 'Do It!'" *St. Paul Dispatch* Newspaper. St. Paul, MN. April 20, 1981. p. 11A.

Chapter Ten

1 Bombeck, Erma. "Youth World Runs on a Small $2 Check." *St. Paul Pioneer Press* Newspaper. St. Paul, MN. June 7, 1981. Accent Section.
2 Langway, Kirsch and Hewitt. "Flying Back to the Nest." *Newsweek* Magazine. April 7, 1980. p. 86.
3 Cary, Lorene. "The Return of the Prodigals." *Time* Magazine. October 13, 1980. p. 118.
4 *Phil Donahue Transcripts #10280.* Air date: 11/18/80. Multimedia Program Productions. Cincinnati, OH. p. 18.
5 Goleman, Daniel. "Leaving Home. Is There a Right Time to Go?" *Psychology Today* Magazine. August, 1980. p. 56.
6 Langway, Kirsch and Hewitt.
7 As cited in Brooks, Andree. "When Married Children Come Home to Live." *New York Times* Newspaper. New York, NY. January 19, 1981. p. B10.
8 Ibid.
9 Weinstein, Grace. "Declaration of Independence." *Glamour* Magazine. August, 1980. p. 64.
10 Ibid.

Author Monica Lauen O'Kane is the mother of eight adult children and lives with her husband and family in a suburb of St. Paul—along with a varying number of nesters.